T0228618

"*With wit and humor and heart-wrenching honesty, Jennifer Probst pens a winner with* Write Naked, *a book for all writers—from the aspirant just sitting down at the keyboard to the multipublished, best-selling author dominating the shelves.* Write Naked *has a place of prominence on my keeper shelf.*"

—J. KENNER, *NEW YORK TIMES* BEST-SELLING AUTHOR

"*Jennifer Probst brings something magical to her writing, and with* Write Naked *she gives you insight into her process. The most important thing a writer can do is hone their process, and this book is a valuable tool to use in doing that.*"

—BOB MAYER, *NEW YORK TIMES* BEST-SELLING AUTHOR

"*Authenticity is the core ingredient of every successful book, and to bring forth the type of raw honesty readers connect to, writers must get naked, placing their own beating heart on the page. Using incredible insight and finesse, Jennifer Probst shows writers how to do this, sharing many valuable lessons from her impressive career along the way. An inspiring read for all levels.*"

—ANGELA ACKERMAN, BEST-SELLING AUTHOR

write naked

Jennifer Probst

WRITER'S
DIGEST
BOOKS

WRITER'S DIGEST BOOKS

An imprint of Penguin Random House LLC
penguinrandomhouse.com

ISBN 978-1-4403-4734-4

Printed in the United States of America

Edited by Cris Freese
Designed by Alexis Estoye

write
naked

Jennifer Probst

WD
WRITER'S
DIGEST
BOOKS

WRITER'S DIGEST BOOKS

An imprint of Penguin Random House LLC
penguinrandomhouse.com

Copyright © 2017 by Jennifer Probst
Penguin Random House supports copyright. Copyright fuels creativity,
encourages diverse voices, promotes free speech, and creates a vibrant culture.
Thank you for buying an authorized edition of this book and for complying
with copyright laws by not reproducing, scanning, or distributing any part of
it in any form without permission. You are supporting writers and allowing
Penguin to continue to publish books for every reader.

ISBN 978-1-4403-4734-4

Printed in the United States of America

Edited by Cris Freese
Designed by Alexis Estoye

dedication

Tribe *(noun).* Definition via the *Oxford Dictionary*: A social division in a traditional society consisting of families or communities linked by social, economic, religious, or blood ties, with a common culture and dialect, typically having a recognized leader.

This book is dedicated to my tribe—my fellow writers.

In my tribe, there is no leader; there is only a group of talented, brave, creative, beautiful souls who believe in the art of writing, and want to make a difference through words. Published, or unpublished, your stories are precious, and the world needs them.

Thank you to the authors whose work I've read in the dark of night. You have comforted me, pushed me, and helped me be brave enough to keep trying; to believe in myself. You have made all the difference.

This book is for you.

acknowledgments

I'd like to tell you a story first.

When I was young, and dreamed of being a published author, there was no Internet or Amazon or anything but bookstores and libraries. If you wanted to learn about the craft of writing, or how to get published, there was one important company that helped you do that.

Writer's Digest.

They distributed *Writer's Digest* magazine, and maintained a book club where you could order books on writing through the mail, or purchase them at local bookstores. I scraped my wages together and bought a subscription to both the magazine and book club. This is how I began to study writing craft. I went to the library to pour over *Writer's Market*—which listed names of agents, editors, and publishers to submit your work. I learned how to write a query letter. I learned how to write a synopsis. It was my Bible.

When I was young, I dreamed about one day being published by Writer's Digest Books. It was an item on my bucket list, kind of like hitting the best-seller list or being successful enough to write full time. I thought if Writer's Digest Books ever wanted to publish me, I'd be a real writer. I'd be important. I'd have something worth saying, and a way to give back to the world of writing.

Thirty years later, this book is getting published.

Dreams do come true.

Thank you to Writer's Digest Books for believing in this book.

Thank you to Cris Freese, my wonderful editor, who loved my voice, fine-tuned it to perfection, and made this book something truly special. It was a pleasure working with you.

Thank you to my agent, Kevan Lyon, who had as much passion for my first work of nonfiction as she does my romance novels. You worked tirelessly trying to find the right home for this book, and I couldn't have done it without you.

about the author

Jennifer Probst wrote her first book at twelve years old. She bound it in a folder, read it to her classmates, and hasn't stopped writing since. She took a short hiatus to get married, get pregnant, buy a house, get pregnant again, pursue a master's in English Literature, and rescue two shelter dogs. Now she is writing again.

She makes her home in Upstate New York with the whole crew. Her sons keep her active, stressed, joyous, and sad that her house will never be truly clean.

She is the *New York Times*, *USA Today*, and *Wall Street Journal* bestselling author of sexy and erotic contemporary romance. She was thrilled her book *The Marriage Bargain* was ranked #6 on Amazon's Best Books for 2012, and spent 26 weeks on the *New York Times*' Best-Seller List. Her work has been translated in over a dozen countries, sold over a million copies, and was nominated for a RITA award. She was dubbed a "romance phenom" by Kirkus Reviews.

She loves hearing from readers. Visit her website for updates on new releases and her street team at www.jenniferprobst.com.

Sign up for her newsletter at www.jenniferprobst.com/newsletter for a chance to win a gift card each month and receive exclusive material and giveaways.

table of contents

PART ONE
being an author

PART TWO
the craft of writing

PART TWO
the craft of writing

Foreword

Being asked to write a Foreword for a book by Jennifer Probst on writing is a pretty sweet gig. Everyone coming into this is just as excited to be here as I am. Writing is the best!

... And also sometimes the worst!

But in those impossible moments when it feels like you're squeezing blood from a brick, or knitting a scarf from a spider web, the amazing writing community reaches out and takes your hand. In this case, the writing community is now placing this resource directly in the palm of your hand.

We consider Jen to be one of the absolute *best* humans in publishing, so I want to personally high five each of you for being smart enough to pick up this book. She has the gift of entertainment—in person, and in her writing—and this guide on craft is no exception.

When she emailed Christina and myself, asking if we would be willing to write a foreword, the conversation went like this:

> Jen: Hey, you two! Would you—
> CLo: Yes.
> Jen: But, I haven't—
> CLo: Doesn't matter. We're in!
> Jen: I'm asking you to write a Foreword.
> CLo: We love Forewords! *Forewords are better than cupcakes.* Everyone reads the Foreword and remembers it *intensely*. In fact, we're already writing and it's basically a love letter to you, and we're all three-way married now.

It's funny—she only communicates through her attorney now.

Now, obviously, we could go on about why she is perfectly suited to write this book. But, if you are a writer (which I assume you are), you likely came here not for accolades and wedding announcements, but for answers to the very common writerly questions, like:

1. Help me?
2. Who let me do this?
3. How do I word?
4. Why does the middle of my book make me sleepy?
5. Why do all my characters sound like me?
6. What are book?

And as such, I can be pretty confident that everyone is wisely skipping my words to get straight to Jen's, because she will answer these questions, and I will not.

And since no one is reading this foreword anyway, I am confident in using this space as a confessional and saying that I was a published author several times over before I ever picked up a book on craft. I like to think that it wasn't hubris so much as an understanding that there is no one way to write a book (a belief that's been validated many times in my experience), and I didn't want another process worming its way into my confidence. If the words are rolling, why change anything? (She said with confidence, at the time.)

I started writing *Days of Our Lives* fan fiction at the age of fourteen, bad poetry at the age of eighteen, and—after the dark years of graduate school—returned once more to fanfic. I didn't study writing—ever. So, much like my son noodling on his guitar—he does different things to his instrument to see what sound comes out—I learned how to write by noodling. Christina and I wrote a book together, and then another, and it sold. People liked it, and so we wrote some more. Books on craft? *Pssh!*

For a while, it seemed to work just fine.

But then I hit a point where the words weren't rolling. Same with Christina. It seemed like we plucked the low-hanging fruit from the

the Idea Tree and *all* of the fruit from the Word Tree, and there was nothing left.

So, to no one's surprise, the next book we wrote had a terrible ending and a middle as mushy as a cranberry bog. Our editor said, "You are both lovely people and make amazing pecan pie, but this book requires a few key strokes: First, Ctrl and A. And then, delete."

So, we picked up *On Writing* by Stephen King, and proceeded to devour every craft book we could get our hands on. They're so much more than *Here's How You Write Real Good*. They're: *Here's How to Think Like a Writer; How to Find Ideas in the Tiny Cracks of Life; How to Put Depth and Dimension in Your Characters; How to Take That Bare Flicker of a Plot Arc and Make It Into a Star Or, At the Very Least, a Really Bright and Useful Flashlight.*

Jen's awesome book won't tell you how to write The End in the one specific manuscript you're struggling to complete. But you don't really want that anyway, because what you're toiling away at is *your book*. What Jen's book will do is give you a tool chest you can internalize and use when you're starting, when you're stuck, when you're editing, and when you just hate every word you've ever written.

There may be sections in here you don't need right now; there may be sections you need but don't realize it yet. There may be advice that validates your current process (because your process is and should be fluid), and I hope that in those moments you take the time to do an air-kick-celebratory-karate-chop combination because you've earned it, badass. There may be chapters that you return to so many times the pages become dog-eared, or your e-reader has been well trained to open to the right page when the app loads. But regardless, this book is here, forever, for *you*.

Look, you're already way ahead of me, because you're reading and seeking guidance, answers, and ideas. Just remember: it's never too early or too late to dive into your craft. Whether you are writing your first book or your fiftieth, you're doing it. Writing can be isolating, but we're all in this together, and I'm excited for you right now. It's how I feel when anyone tells me they've never watched Alias, never read *The*

Captive Prince, or never eaten a Sprinkles triple cinnamon cupcake, because I can say, *You have this wonderful experience ahead of you!*

You, lucky writer, have this wonderful book ahead of you.

(Your own book, and the one you're currently holding in your hands.)

Go forth, and conquer!

xoxo
Christina Lauren

Introduction

"The creator made us creative. Our creativity is our gift from God. Our use of it is our gift to God. Accepting this bargain is the beginning of true self-acceptance."

—JULIA CAMERON, *THE ARTIST'S WAY*

This is not a book that will help you earn a million dollars with your writing.

This is not a book to teach you how to edit your writing, publish your book, gain tons of followers on Twitter and Facebook, or crack Amazon's top 100.

This is a book for writers. For all writers. Whether you write full-time, part-time, as a hobby, or even if you simply dream of writing one day, this book will strip down the layers of this fascinating career, examine all aspects of writing, and try to help you blast through any blocks you have about writing.

I'm sure you're wondering why I'm qualified to write such a book. What makes me an expert?

I don't claim to have all the answers, but I've written this book for a variety of reasons. I've published over twenty-five books and written over thirty-five. My work includes all formats: an eighty-one-word story, a novella, an essay, and both short and full-length novels. I hold a master's degree in English Literature. I have experienced the lowest of lows and incredible highs, from writing in near poverty to exploding onto *The New York Times* best-seller list and staying there for over twenty-six weeks. I've been published by both traditional publishers and digital publishers, and I have experience in self-publishing.

I have a deep love for the written word in all forms, even the 140-character tweet. Writing is my passion; it's the great love of my life. And I've found craft books to be food for my soul: I've steeped myself in the various voices, advice, and analysis of writers like Stephen King, Natalie Goldberg, Anne Lamott, Julia Cameron, Blake Snyder, Chuck Wendig, Jane Yolen, Steven Pressfield, William Zinsser, Annie Dillard, and so many others. I believe my writing muse gets to take a deep breath and reset when I read these books. Sometimes, in the mad scramble for publication—finishing our books, formatting, editing, marketing, promoting, and the thousand other tasks it takes to be a writer in today's world—we need to step back and rediscover what being a writer is.

So I invite you to step into these pages, take a breath, and delve into your writing life, in all its forms. Rediscover what it is to be a writer. The chapters are easy to skim if you feel like jumping around, and I have included many personal stories, along with the advice of best-selling authors in a chapter called "Trademarks of Best-Selling Authors." But my main goal in writing this book was to try and give back to the career I love.

So, let's begin.

Let's talk about being a writer.

"If you are going through hell, keep going."

—WINSTON CHURCHILL

write naked

PART ONE

being

an

author

1

beginnings

"Begin at the beginning and go on till you come to the end: then stop."

—LEWIS CARROLL

When I begin writing a book, I'm both awestruck and humbled at the power of a blank page. The endless possibilities and expectations are overwhelming. There's joy in being able to take a slice of who you are and translate it into words. And there's a crippling fear of the snowy, blinding white blizzard of emptiness, page after crisp page with no limitations except the human mind and imagination.

Beginnings—those first words, filling the emptiness—are important.

I have spoken to countless writers who approach a new project in a variety of ways. Some jump in, half-cocked, fearless, and determined to conquer the story. Others dip a toe in, test the waters, write a few sentences, then take their time to ease all the way in. There's also a third type: those who stare at that blinking cursor, paralyzed and numb, knowing *this is it*. This is where everyone realizes you're a fraud. You can't do it again, you can't do it as well, or this idea will suck once you commit it to paper. The spiral of thoughts take over the natural inclination until hours pass and nothing is written.

Despite that potential fear, beginnings are necessary.

We need beginnings to function. Beginnings are a New Year's resolution: whether it's the start of a new day, week, or year; whether it's a graduation or birth or even death. Beginnings set the tone of the story and can change at any time. All it takes is a decision to change. And the commitment to follow it through.

I've been a writer since I was six years old. I'm one of the lucky ones, discovering my passion and True North while kids around me talked about being princesses and cowboys or astronauts. The moment I picked up a book, something inside me shifted, as if it were all so very familiar. My mother said I read voraciously at a very young age and all I ever wanted was to be left alone in my room with a stack of books.

I scribbled nonstop in journals and diaries. I crafted essays on my life, which didn't include much at the time except for my love of books, my struggle in a new school, and my dog.

At twelve, I decided to write my first full-length novel. It was a young adult romance, written in longhand, bound in a yellow folder. I wrote every day without fail. It took me ten months to write that book, and I carried it to school and read it to my classmates in junior high.

By then I was hooked.

I graduated to a Brother Typewriter and penned my second romance, headphones covering my ears, carving out my space at the end of the rarely used dining room table. I twisted my angst and dreams into fictional characters on the page, realizing even then that my writing style consisted of a little truth and a lot of lies. After my third book, which I was brave enough to submit to a young writer's contest, I was already thinking of a sequel.

Writers discover their calling at different times in their lives. Some learn it at an early age, while others fall into it due to circumstance or from an unfulfilled craving for creativity. Some write to prove they can do better than others. Others write because there is a desperate need to tell a particular story, one that's caged inside them. It's important to remember how we began and to honor the fork in the road that brought us to writing. Like honoring our individual birth stories, our earliest writing days should mean something.

I'm also a firm believer that everyone is already born to write. We are instinctually driven to remember, to share our stories, to be known in this world to someone. Writing is the most personal, truthful way of expressing our stories to the world—even if we are writing fiction. Our writing voice is unique to us, even when that voice may be still raw and unformed.

Writing gives us a slice of immortality, a trail of bread crumbs for the people who follow us. Our writing tells readers that we loved, cried, feared, and experienced pain. We were important. This is what we saw and this is how we showed the world our personal view of what it is to be human and alive.

I'm always amazed at the passionate way children and teens write. They are in touch with their emotions, and can tap into joy and pain more freely. Emotions are more real to them—age, society, and expectations haven't yet anesthetized them. Their stories are full of imagination and depth. And by committing stories to the page, they allow those stories to live and breathe, and they can begin to figure those stories out.

I was lucky enough to be invited to a local elementary school to speak with fourth graders about being a full-time writer. After informing the class that the greatest benefits were working in my pajamas and getting to make things up for fun—including killing anyone who pissed me off—I asked if they enjoyed writing. Almost every single hand shot up in the air. Then I asked them if they ever wrote something—a story, a poem, an essay, a letter. Everyone raised their hand. I informed the group they were all "real" writers.

A sea of excited faces stared back at me. One little girl burst out, "But I don't get paid!"

Sigh. Yep. I didn't get paid either for a *long* time.

Did that mean my work at the time was not valuable? That I wasn't a true writer? Sure, my writing didn't pay my bills, but my writing helped me make sense of my life. With every word I wrote, I learned more. I improved. I built discipline. And, eventually, I paid my bills.

I told the class that if they put words to paper, and they do it with true intention, they are writers. I told them the teachers were there to help their craft and improve their writing, but no one could take away their original ideas or their unique ways of expressing them. If you put one hundred people in a room and ask them to write a story on one subject, you won't get two stories that sound exactly the same.

My son's teacher called me later that afternoon. She said they threw out their class schedule for the day after my speech. Instead each child wrote a story. The class was more enthusiastic and excited than the teacher had ever seen, and the students asked if I could come back and hear their tales.

My son came home that week with three chapter books written by his classmate. His friend started a series after realizing that his dream was possible—even at a young age.

I'm sure I'll see his published works in the future.

I've voraciously read books on writing since I was young. I thirsted for other writers' knowledge, whether that was craft, marketing, or exploring the writing life. I didn't feel so alone when I read them.

Hearing the intimate thoughts, viewpoints, and advice of writers fed my soul and helped me grow. It still does. I have learned my own truths in my writing journey over the years.

These are the truths I want to share with you, but there is one that ranks above all others.

Writing is essentially done alone.

I didn't have the Internet then and a mass of information wasn't available, but even in today's noisy, chaotic, and bustling society, writing is still done alone. The writer. The pen or keyboard. The paper or computer. The mind and soul and imagination. Nothing more, nothing less.

I explain this truth in various ways throughout these chapters, but not as well as the following piece, brilliantly written by Michael Ventura. Writers continuously struggle for the right words to communicate the vivid perfection of thought or idea—that's the goal when one sits down to write. When I first read "The Talent of the Room," I realized Ventura succeeded in truly understanding what it meant to be a writer. It doesn't matter what stage of writing you've reached—whether beginner or advanced—there is one element to be faced every day: the room.

I've reprinted it here, with his permission. I'm honored to share the piece as it has helped me truly understand what it is to be a writer.

"THE TALENT OF THE ROOM" BY MICHAEL VENTURA

Letters at 3 a.m. – 1993 © Michael Ventura.
Used with the author's generous permission.
Originally published in LA Weekly, 21-27 May 1993
http://michaelventura.org/the-talent-of-the-room-1993/

People who are young at writing—and this does not necessarily mean they're young in years—ask me, now and again, if I can tell them something useful about the task. Task is my word, not theirs, and it may seem a harsh and formal word, but before writing is anything else it's a task. Only gradually do you learn enough for it to become a craft. (As for whether writing becomes your art—that isn't really up to you. The art can be there in the beginning, before you know a thing, or it may never be there no matter what you learn.)

"The only thing you really need," I tell these people, "is the talent of the room. Unless you have that, your other talents are worthless."

Writing is something you do alone in a room. Copy that sentence and put it on your wall because there's no way to exaggerate or overemphasize this fact. It's the most important thing to remember if you want to be a writer. Writing is something you do alone in a room.

Before any issues of style, content or form can be addressed, the fundamental questions are: How long can you stay in that room? How many hours a day? How do you behave in that room? How often can you go back to it? How much fear (and, for that matter, how much elation) can you endure by yourself? How many years—how many years—can you remain alone in a room?

I know people who, when young, had wonderful talents: prose of grace and resonance that came without effort, sentences that moved intelligently with that crucial element of surprise, never concluding quite where one expected, so that you were always eager to read the next and the next. Promising work as they say. But to write anything that would keep the promise, to go beyond the letters, verse and stories of their youth, written with such enthusiasm, friends and teachers praising them, little magazines publishing them—to take the next step meant that they would have to sit alone in a room for years.

Some sat just for weeks. Some lasted months. Some kept saying that next summer, or next winter, or after they graduated, or when they moved to

write naked

Europe (which they never did), or when they got a grant, or when they weren't so busy, or when they could afford a place that gave them the space (because they needed an actual room; it couldn't be just the bedroom or the kitchen)... sometime in the foreseeable but not the immediate future, then they'd write the novel or complete that sequence of poems.

A few of these talented people would even arrange the room. A good desk, a clean well-oiled typewriter (a computer now), the paper, the pencils, the stereo, maybe a hot plate. But after the room is ready you have to sit in it. For a very long time. (Sometimes it takes weeks or months even to begin writing.) And that's the talent they didn't have.

There's no harm or blame in not having a talent. But it is very painful to have some of the talents, almost all of the talents, except the one you really need.

* * *

The teachers who fawn on your early work (if you were lucky or unlucky enough, as the case may be, to have such teachers) don't usually tell you about this because they're not writers, they're teachers. They may do some writing on the side, but few have staked their lives on writing. Their wages, their prestige, their social life, their surroundings, the rhythms of their days and of their years, are rooted in the profession of teaching, which is an activity done in a room with other people, surrounded by rooms filled with people, upstairs and downstairs and down the hall. You cannot teach the demands of solitude in such places. Even if you talk about it, you're not teaching it—the surroundings contradict the lesson.

The surroundings always are the lesson. That's the trouble with college. What it teaches, more than anything else, is how to go to college. Thus most writing courses, by their very nature, ignore the fundamental thing you need to be a writer. That's why, although thousands teach such courses and tens of thousands attend them, precious little work results. You'll notice that the ratio of teaching to work accomplished is much better in med school or in truck driver's school, because those involve skills that can be taught.

Nobody can teach you how you, in particular, are going to behave when you're alone for hours a day over long periods of time trying to deal with unknown quantities: what you have to express, what experience your expression draws on, how that experience relates to the solitude necessary for its expression, the form in which it comes out (which is never quite the form you planned on), how that form changes as it progresses, and, most important, who you are—all these are just a few of the unknown quantities that are locked up with you in your room.

If you're Sharon Doubiago, your room is your van; if you're the young Ernest Hemingway, your room is a café table; if you're Emily Dickinson, your room is your garden; if you're Marcel Proust, you write in bed; if you're William Faulkner, you compose *As I Lay Dying* in six weeks in a humid shack while you work days in a factory (or was it work nights and write days?). But whoever you are, whatever shape it takes, that room is the center of your life and it's very crowded. Everything you are and everything you're not backs you up against the wall and stares at you. You stare back. And eventually you get some writing done.

The thing about the room is this: it's likely you'll have to remain there for years before you even know whether or not you're any good—and it may be years more before anyone else knows. Because you can have the talent of the room and can spend years there but still not be much of a writer. Or twenty years can go by and you are good, but you don't get published; or you get published, but nobody notices; or they notice, but they hate it; or you're a lousy writer, but they love it and you get rich. Whatever. The only thing you know you'll have twenty years down the line is the experience of the room—how you behaved, what you felt, what you thought, what you dared, what you fled, how you lived life, how life lived you, alone, in that room.

Remember, even if you're financially successful at writing, and even if success comes early, you still have to spend the rest of your life in that room. Money and recognition make many things easier, but they don't change the basic conditions of writing. You may furnish the room better, but you still have to enter it alone and stay there until something happens. And if your livelihood and your family's well-being now depend upon your behavior in that room, then the quality of that behavior becomes crucial in many new ways. Your honesty, your originality, even the accuracy of your memory may very well become financial liabilities.

Most people can blame their sellouts on the institutions they work for, or on the way everybody else does business, or on the political climate, or whatever. The vast majority of us are simply hired to do a job and then ordered to cut corners, and we feel we have little choice. But nobody orders anybody to become a writer. And nobody becomes a writer without dreams of glory and art. Writers do their selling out consciously, alone in their rooms, where they can't help but know what they're doing, adjusting sentence after sentence to what's saleable, to what the publishers or the editors or the studios want.

It takes a while for those adjustments to become reflexes—a long while of whittling away what's best in yourself. When the process is over you have a face to match it, which is why most screenwriters and freelancers look the way they do.

* * *

When it's all over, if you've stuck and had some luck, you have a few things published that you're proud of and a pretty good idea of who you are. Without the first you probably wouldn't have stayed in the room so long, and without the second you'd have gone crazy a long time ago. Crazy as a writer would define it: too unbalanced to work. If you can still write, then how crazy can you be?

Plenty crazy, is the answer. The room can become a hole. Your talent of the room, your ability to be there with all your soul, can overwhelm you. Then the rest of life becomes unreal and, worse than unreal, a kind of un-life. So you find yourself writing with a very sophisticated consciousness but living in your relationships with other people far beneath what you write, because it's gotten so you only really exist in that room and you don't care about outside. And since you write necessarily from memory—for writing in a sense is memory, is what you cared about yesterday, or last month, or in your childhood—your lack of feeling for the present may not show up in your work for a while. But when it does, you're through. You may still be published, still make money, still be read, but people won't care the way they used to—and they'll know it, and they'll let you know it.

The room, you see, is a dangerous place. Not in itself, but because you're dangerous. The psyche is dangerous. Because working with words is not like working with color or sound or stone or movement. Color and sound and stone and movement are all around us, they are natural elements, they've always been in the universe, and those who work with them are servants of these timeless materials. But words are pure creations of the human psyche. Every single word is full of secrets, full of associations. Every word leads to another and another and another, down and down, through passages of dark and light. Every single word leads, in this way, to the same destination: your soul. Which is, in part, the soul of everyone. Every word has the capacity to start that journey. And once you're on it, there is no knowing what will happen.

Locking yourself up with such things, letting them stir, using these pure psychic creations as raw material, and deciding, each time, how much or little you're going to participate in your own act of creation, just what you'll stake, what are the odds, just how far are you going to go—that's called being a writer. And you do it alone in a room.

It doesn't matter what type of writer you are—whether you have a story lodged in your heart, clawing to escape, or you are a full timer with a dozen manuscripts behind you. It doesn't matter if you're a seasoned veteran or working on your first project. You are a writer because you write. Because you have something to say. Because you are alive, and want to share or work out what burns within your soul—both good and bad.

So, together, let's do the most important thing a writer can do.

Let's begin.

·······························*Exercise*·····························

Take some time to remember and write down what you know about your birth. Birth stories tell us how we came into the world and may hold a mysterious key to how we look at life. Sketch the details of your story, whether it's happy, sad, or painful.

Now, remember the first time you decided to write. Journal about how it made you feel, what you wrote, and what your experience was. Don't judge yourself—this is an exercise in exploration; there is no good or bad. Read it over. Then let it go, because right now, in this moment, it's your new beginning and the story you want to tell.

···

2

write naked

"*Motives get lost in the passage of time, subject to the ravages of memory and revisionism. What stays—and therefore what matters—is what you do.*"

—NEIL ABRAMSON, *UNSAID*

As a multipublished writer of romance fiction, I get asked about sex a lot.

Is this the chapter we discuss it?

No.

We'll get to sex later.

Writing naked is the necessary state of mind for translating the mess of raw material in your brain into words on a page. Most people think you need to be able to make sense of the junk first. You don't. Instead you need to *feel* it, *connect* with it, and then *write* it. The mess is the structure and meat of the story. Even if you are composing a love letter, the best way to connect is to spill your deepest, darkest, embarrassing secrets. Reveal the stuff that terrifies you and keeps you awake at night. Talk about the monsters in the closet, and the ones hiding under the bed. Get in touch with the kind of emotions that drive the fear of abandonment, failure, and pain.

This is the good stuff.

A reader wants to feel something. A reader doesn't want to be intellectually stimulated or to be able to skillfully talk about your work in a book club. She doesn't want to check off your book on her list of smart reads, feeling nothing but mild admiration for your writing expertise.

Failure to connect on an emotional level with a reader is the kiss of death for a writer.

I want a reader to pick up my stuff and get dirty. I want her turned on during the sex scenes, choked up during the black moment, and blinking tears at the ending. (The black moment is what happens when the hero or heroine needs to change, or risk losing the other forever.) I want her yelling at the page because of the asshole hero and laughing out loud at the characters' banter. Hell, I'd rather have a reader say she *hated* my book (many have on Goodreads—and, yes, it still hurts), than be apathetic toward it. I'd rather her say she loathed it, wanted to rip it up, and tell every one of her friends to never ever read me again. At least that's passion. I may have missed the mark, but I got the emotion right. Lukewarm comments are the worst insult to the success-driven writer. *Okay. Fine. An average read.*

Kill me now.

Trust me, you don't want to pat yourself on the back for sounding smart, cool, or savvy in your writing. The best way to connect with your real self is to get naked. Strip your soul bare and throw it out there. Don't try to make sense of it until the ink dries, because you can always go back and tweak, tidy things up, or edit, which we'll talk about later.

When I finished *Searching for Beautiful*, I was a wreck. I had to quickly turn around and start my newest book to make my deadline, but I felt emotionally drained and unable to connect with another character for a while. My characters haunted me, keeping me up at night. I told them over and over to go away, that their story was finally done, to just leave me the hell alone so I could get some much-needed sleep. But they didn't. I heard their voices, and their story lingered in my fingertips as I tried to dive into my next project. My newest hero seemed just a flicker of a personality. My heroine had the same characteristics as my previous one. I couldn't move on, and I didn't know why this book affected me so deeply.

After a long talk with my editor, I had my lightbulb moment. *Searching for Beautiful* was about a runaway bride who was in an abusive relationship. The novel had flickers of truth from my own past. I married someone I shouldn't have—someone who was emotionally abusive—but I never ran out on my wedding. Fighting my own panic attack, I sucked it up and married him. We divorced within six months. It was an emotionally painful experience and I had many regrets. Why hadn't I cancelled the wedding? Why hadn't I been brave enough? What would have happened if I had run away, blown up my life, and watched the pieces scatter?

I realized that was the theme of *Searching for Beautiful*. My heroine flees her wedding through a church window—because her gut screams for her to run. I didn't listen. But she did.

I was able to play out those what-ifs in my fictional world, but doing so left me vulnerable. I opened up old wounds, examined them, and explored. The book reeks of emotion because I poured myself into the story.

My editor advised me to read the finished book one last time, as a reader, to fully grasp the emotional journey I'd travelled. When I reached the end, I was finally able to put my past to rest and move on to my next story. I needed to experience my own sense of closure with the characters before I was truly able to take on new ones.

Many experts in the writing field advise us to write what we know. When you write naked, you're doing this each time, allowing the reader a glimpse of yourself.

Not everyone is going to like who you are. That's one of the hardest parts of the business. But not everyone is supposed to like you all the time. By practicing the act of writing naked, you will begin to connect with your true voice and touch readers on an emotional level.

Great books have great emotion. I'll talk more about writing emotion in a future chapter. But in order to get there, you need to write naked. Strip to your bare skin and write your book in the glorious, raw mess just as nature intended. You can sort out the good stuff from the junk later. But when you're writing that first draft, you need to go for it.

I always remember that scene from *Romancing the Stone* where the heroine, Joan, is shown as a successful romance writer. She was finishing her book, writing the final scene, and weeping uncontrollably over her desk.

When I finish a book, I always cry. It's my own sign of realizing it's good, that I've given it everything I had, and the foundation is firm enough not to crumble under any edits.

Right or wrong, that's how I know I'm writing naked. It may get a bit chilly, and a whole lot vulnerable, but the result will be worth it.

That result is the best book you can possibly deliver, and that is what every reader should expect from you.

You are naked when you share your work—make no doubt about it. The good news is you will become more and more comfortable without your clothes the longer you write. There's something freeing and wild about telling the world the way you see things.

When you sit down to create, you must be brave enough to rid yourself of societal expectations and the crushing cliques civilization force on us. You may hurt and embarrass your family. You may need to hide your books from your children. You may find people from your past rise up to confront, judge, or mock you. You may face harsh reviews from a world that wags its finger and admonishes you to *get dressed* and write nicely. Fully clothed.

But great risks mean great rewards. When people are asked about their regrets in life, they often list the things they didn't do. The book they were afraid to write because it wouldn't sell, or because the writing was too difficult, or because they were too busy doing things that were safe or marketable.

Writing naked is the only way to write. And as a writer, your only regret will be looking back and realizing you wrote with a giant fur coat, boots, and—horror of horrors—too tight underwear.

Burn the bra. Burn the boxers. Burn the regrets.

Write naked.

·····························*Exercise*·····························

Take off all your clothes ... nah, just kidding! Write about an event that was extremely personal to you. Just grab your notebook and let it rip. This is for your eyes only. Make sure you go deep and expose everything you felt during that moment. Read it over, and see if you can connect to the experience. This isn't about grammar, spelling, or well-constructed sentences. This is about the emotion on the page and how it feels reading your story.

During your next writing project, try to remember what it felt like to write something deeply personal without any barriers between you and the reader. The more you practice writing naked, the easier it gets.

. . . .

3

writers are crazy

'Don't try to figure out what other people want to hear from you; figure out what you have to say. It's the one and only thing you have to offer.'

—BARBARA KINGSOLVER

The writing life comes with a lot of assumptions.

Some are outdated; some have never been put to rest. Let's go over a few, shall we?

Many famous writers have been known to struggle with alcoholism, depression, suicide, and a host of other ailments. We have the ghost of Hemingway with us—the ultimate artist and alcoholic, driven to commit suicide. But other authors have struggled, battling addiction: Virginia Woolf, Anne Sexton, F. Scott Fitzgerald, Edgar Allan Poe, William Faulkner, Hunter S. Thompson, and James Joyce. Even Stephen King admitted his battle with alcohol and writing.

Personally, I'm deathly afraid to see if I write better when I'm drinking. It would be dangerous if I decided the answer was yes. My father is an alcoholic, and I know the demons that can haunt me if my love for a good glass of wine turns into more, especially if I find writing becomes easier that way. Better to keep Pandora's box shut and not find out.

Though I still like my wine.

Many great artists find it difficult to live with such creativity and brilliance; it's hard for them to lead what we call a normal life. Smoking, drinking, drugs, sex, excess partying, all of it can be a way to silence the muse that churns incessantly in our heads. Of course, it can also drive us to self-destruction.

Still, we have a choice. Just as we choose to sit down and write every day, we can choose to have brief moments of brilliance and endless moments of misery. I treat my writing career like everything else I do in this life: an opportunity to work hard, grow, learn, hope for a little luck, and keep on going. Never quit. I may never create a book that lives on for decades, but I will have lived a full life, doing my damn best on a daily basis.

Sometimes being a writer is just as boring as being an office worker. We show up, sit our butts in the chair, and do the work. There are good days and bad days. There are two thousand–word days that are crap, and one thousand–word days of sheer brilliance. Sometimes we make money; many times we don't. But writing is a better life because of what we decide to do with our talent. I'd rather bow to a creative higher power than the lure of temporary fixes that may destroy the delicate creative balance. We do not need to cloak artistic brilliance in drugs, alcohol, depression, or other negative behaviors. There are many people who struggle with these battles who do not work full-time in the creative arts. Such assumptions— that writers are crazy—can end up being dangerous.

Besides being dubbed as self-destructive, the public also likes to portray a writer as a tortured, brooding artist who needs constant inspiration and the perfect atmosphere to actually write the book. This artist is wonderful at acting like a writer, but the words put on paper are usually too few. You've met them. They complain about lack of time and the widespread misunderstanding within the industry. They dismiss bad reviews with their nose stuck up in the air: "The reader *just didn't get it.*" They are great at describing what they're writing, but we rarely see results. This is simply acting. Not writing.

The intention to write in one's spare time does not make someone a true author. I call this the wannabe writer. These are people who clap me on the back, nod understandingly, and tell me if they only had the time, they'd write their own book. But, of course, it's so hard with normal responsibilities and real jobs. They don't think writing is difficult, and in their mind, they don't really think writing a book is a big deal. In fact, I think they believe that a great idea (if they even have one) is as good as having actually written the book.

I can't tell you how many times people sport a curious frown after I tell them I'm a writer. Then they ask me, "So after you write, you have the whole day free?"

Umm. Sure. After my ten-hour workday, I'm free as a bird.

I've met all these types, but I'll tell you one thing I've discovered: The writers who are real—the writers who *write*—all have one thing in common. They're crazy. Loony tunes. They've got a screw loose. Whackadoo. Pick your favorite.

I mean, let's be honest, how can we not be? We talk to imaginary people. We fret and worry over the characters in our head; people who often feel more real than the ones here on Earth. We fight with them, cry with them, and try to make them move on the page, even when they refuse.

I had a painter who came to work on my house for five days. The first day, he kept stopping his work and showing up at my office door, a puzzled expression on his face because he'd thought he'd heard me yelling for him. Each time, I'd say no. On the second day, he didn't even bother to check. By then he knew that I talk to myself and my dog in real, lengthy conversations about my book. I mutter. I ponder. I yell. And the only one who's there to listen is my dog. This is my normal.

Writers are always gathering information for their stories. For example, I tend to eavesdrop on conversations. My husband gets upset when I linger at tables in restaurants because I need to know how a stranger's problems resolve. Once we stayed an extra half hour in a booth at a diner because the couple behind us was fighting about a girl he may or may not have kissed—he swore he didn't—and his girlfriend was deciding whether or not they could still be together. I ordered two desserts just so I could stay longer.

See, writers view the world in a different way. The world is a story, our own personal playground. I've heard doctors have incredible egos because they are *playing* God by saving someone's life.

Writers *are* God. We create people readers believe are real.

Writers are also solitary. I don't care how many conferences you go to or how many online friends you chat with. When you write, you are alone. No one can do the work for you, or with you.

I spend hours by myself, with my imaginary worlds and characters. I don't wear real pants. I live in pajamas. I own hundreds of shoes but never wear them. When I drag myself outside to pick up my kids at school, everyone is embarrassed. It's almost as if I don't remember how to function in the real world: the polite chitchat, makeup, and those damn shoes. I just stand there like a guppy, confused by fresh air, my head stuffed with cotton balls as I try to transition away from my book. I look like a homeless person on a regular basis. My boys are starting to ask me if they can take the bus.

And I am very rarely at a comfortable place in my career. Ever. This is because of the constant transition a full-time writing career entails. I'm always working on a new story, editing a previous one, or promoting my newest release. Usually, it's a combination of the three under the pressure of a regular deadline I'm sure I'll miss.

Since my work revolves around imaginary people, this also becomes a challenge in the evening. In the bedroom. I keep a terrible secret from my husband. It is never just us in our bed. Between us is always my newest hero. I've learned to accept it as a way of life. When I'm writing about a new hero, I'm madly in love with him—every bit of him, including his faults. And my alpha males have many faults. This, unfortunately, transfers to the way in which I treat my husband. If I'm forgiving my hero for the terrible things he's doing, I don't have the patience to forgive my husband at the same time. So I yell and sigh and tell my husband to be better, *dammit!* How can I possibly be expected to forgive two unruly males?

Yep. *Crazy.*

Here's the secret, though: Don't accept the crazy; *embrace it.* It's wonderful to be different. The moment those voices stop in my head, I no longer know who I am. I know how my friends roll their eyes when I glaze over in line and suddenly forage desperately for a pen and scrap of paper to write down an idea. I know people laugh when they hear I once went grocery shopping and ended up across town because I was wrapped up in plotting my book and missed the store. That's what being a writer is.

I pretend to be a real person, but I'm really just a mess, trying to be normal enough to fit into society.

But writers are also amazingly brave and true to themselves, because it takes strength and purpose and guts to decide you're going to write a story for people to read.

Writing is a way of sticking it to everyone who has ever judged you not worthy, belittled your creativity, or thought of you as weird. It's a way of balancing things, sifting through who you are, who you want to be, and who you will decide to be.

Embrace the crazy. Because, honestly, one of the worst horrors in the world, is being called normal.

································*Exercise*································

Take a moment to look over your life and think about the times creativity has come into play. How did it make you feel? How did you act? Did you try to change your creativity by being logical? Have you been happier in times when you listened to your crazy thoughts, or did you have regrets? Without judgment, connect with some of your past experiences of creativity in your life's journey. Write them down in a notebook. This is a good time, as a writer, to make intentions to decide what you need more or less of.

4

green with envy

"The truth, revealed by action in the direction of our dreams, is that there is room for all of us. But jealousy produces tunnel vision. It narrows our ability to see things in perspective. It strips us of our ability to see other options. The biggest lie that jealousy tells us is that we have no choice but to be jealous. Perversely, jealousy strips us of our will to act when action holds the key to our freedom."

—JULIA CAMERON, *THE ARTIST'S WAY*

This was a hard chapter to write. Mostly because I had to be brutally honest and share a few things I'd rather not invite the world to see. But this book is titled *Write Naked* for a reason. If I'm not ready to get messy and real, what's the point?

I've had a difficult time with envy. I'm not proud of it. When readers see this, there's going to be a lot of shock, because I hide it quite well. I'm also going to give advice that may not be politically correct. But I'll tell the truth.

As humans, we all experience envy. Jealousy. I try to separate them in a way that makes it clear.

First, I looked up the definitions and found envy and jealousy, by definition, to be pretty much the same. But we can use it differently in our writing to reflect a personal choice.

Since this is my book, I'm claiming my right to show how I perceive the difference between envy and jealousy, and how I guide myself through the maze of mess.

ENVY: Simply put, you really, really want what your neighbor has, but you don't hate your neighbor. She can have it, no problem. In fact, you *want* her to have it, but you want it for yourself, too. Can't we all just be happy together?

JEALOUSY: Basically, you want what your neighbor has, but you are pissed that your neighbor has what you have wanted forever. You worked so damn hard to attain it, but still don't have it, and you secretly think they don't even deserve it. You want to take it. You don't want your neighbor to have it. You want it for yourself.

Knowing the difference is key. Sometimes I can soothe myself by admitting I'm experiencing envy, but I've not stooped to the primitive, awful emotions of jealousy yet.

It also makes rational sense. If your good friend wins a million dollars, you are over the moon happy for her. *But* you really want a million dollars, too. You'll experience some discomfort with being envious of your friend, but you don't want to take that million dollars away from her.

Now, let's gift that million dollars to an enemy. Say you hate your next-door neighbor. You think she's obnoxious, entitled, and arrogant. You hear she won a million dollars and your first reaction is rage. How could she possibly be rich? She's not a good person. You're better than her. You deserve a million dollars more, because you'd share it, help the world, and be modest about it. Now the jealousy hits hard, and you seethe with this poison that seeps into your veins and keeps turning over and over in your mind.

I have spent my life trying to be grateful for what I have. I learned the lessons well from my own mother. I was also raised in a strict Catholic household. I attended Bible classes, religious instruction, and church every Sunday. When my girlfriend would hold sleepovers, I was the one

write naked

forced to leave at the crack of dawn to attend church, my mother beeping for me in the driveway. I resented my Catholic upbringing for a long time. I hated church. It was boring. I often felt guilty, sitting there as I used that time to fantasize about kissing or sex scenes from my latest book or story. Sometimes I wondered if the altar would blow up due to my irreverence.

But I learned something very important from my religion. We were supposed to follow the Ten Commandments stringently. And one of them is "Thou shalt not covet thy neighbor's wife." When I asked for further explanation, I received an in-depth lesson on envy and jealousy.

Once, when my friend got a really cool Smurfs toy that my parent's couldn't afford, I was envious. And when my fake friend got picked as the National Spelling Bee contestant and pretended to be sad for me, I was jealous.

But covetousness wasn't the only commandment I wanted to break. We were supposed to attend church services every Sunday, but I hated it, and I swore I'd stop attending when I was old enough to make that decision for myself. My mother, shocked and appalled, asked me why I didn't want to go to church. I told her I was bored and got nothing out of it. I didn't feel close to God, and I didn't feel transformed when I left church. I only felt pissed off that I'd lost an hour of my weekend.

One Sunday I received a sermon from our priest, one that has served me quite well over the years. He spoke about serving God. He told a story about a man who prayed to God on his knees, on a hard, cold floor, day after day after day. Another man always joined him, doing the same.

After weeks, the priest asked both men about their experiences praying. The first man told him he felt transformed by prayer. He swore he never experienced the physical discomfort of sore knees or legs. He loved every moment of it.

The second man said he felt nothing. He complained about the pains in his legs, the creak in his bones, and the cold in the air. He said by the time he was done praying, he could only hobble out of the church. He said he didn't know if God was there—he never sensed a light, God speaking to him, or a sign he was doing the right thing. He confessed the prayer session was very difficult for him.

The priest asked the congregation which man was closer to God. Imagine my surprise when he explained it was the second man. Why?

Because he was honest. Praying sucked. But he loved God, and he did it anyway. Day after day after day, no matter what happened. No matter what didn't happen.

The priest said he was accomplishing something very important for a man of faith.

He faked it till he made it.

He may not have felt anything, but he showed up. He went through the motions until enough time had passed that the pain dulled and praying became a habit.

We may not feel a certain way, but we can certainly act a certain way. God didn't judge the man by what he felt or didn't feel. God appreciated that this man showed up to pray, rain or shine, happy or angry. He went through the motions to show his intention of faith.

Would the man who prayed faithfully continue on a regular basis if he stopped sensing God's presence? Did he have the moxie to continue, or would it be easy to abandon when he stopped getting the results he wanted?

I'm not sure.

How does this story relate to this chapter?

When I experience a bolt of raw, primal jealousy, I make sure my actions are positive in order to contradict the negative emotion.

Here's an example: When I was just starting out, I had a lot of publishers interested in my books, but at that time, they'd keep my manuscripts for months before deciding to reject or accept the book. I had an acquaintance who seemed to be at the same crossroads. She was close to getting "the call," just as I was. We wrote for similar markets and both of us have strong voices.

One day, she got the call. I was envious, but I wished her well. She began regularly publishing books and building popularity.

I racked up more rejection letters.

I began to obsess. I'd read her books and truly believed mine were just as good. Why wasn't I getting published? Then one day, her book was the top pick for a popular book club, and suddenly, her career skyrocketed.

It was a true Cinderella story. Her books were everywhere: airports, bookstores, featured in magazines. She received great press and fabulous reviews. She became the darling of the romance world, and as I watched her career explode beyond reach, I began to feel something worse than envy.

Jealousy.

My obsession grew. I let the bad feelings twist and turn inside, until I felt like I could burst. Suddenly it didn't matter where I was in my career, because I'd never be her. I wasted valuable time comparing our careers, worrying about mine, and getting angry over something I wanted to feel joyful about. Things continued to spiral, as I received more rejections and realized she'd be a famous author and I'd be a failure.

I'm not proud of my feelings, but they were real. And then I realized another thing. I couldn't keep living like that. I felt overshadowed, as if nothing I did was good enough, but this writer had done nothing to deserve my inner wrath. She deserved my support. She had proven that hard work and perseverance are rewarded in time. She paved the way for everyone and showed me that anything was possible if you never, ever quit.

So I decided to do something to turn the tides of my dark emotions. I went out and bought her books. I wrote her an e-mail congratulating her. I supported her in social groups and referred her books to friends.

My actions contradicted my feelings. I turned bad into good. I faked it until I made it.

Eventually it happened. The bad stuff eased, and I saw past the ugliness. Finally, I could concentrate on my journey. And now I use this lesson time and time again when jealousy shakes my foundation and leaves me helpless and embarrassed.

I want to be a good person. I believe I am a good person. But occasionally, I am only human.

If you ever find yourself crippled by jealousy, or even depressed from reading everyone's perfect and happy Facebook status, take these steps:

1. **ACKNOWLEDGE.** Denying how you feel is useless. Just own up, even if it's hard. These are your own private feelings and if you feel mean, whiney, and pissed off that you didn't get what *she* got, just go with it.
2. **ACT IN A WAY THAT CONTRADICTS THE FEELINGS.** If there's a particular author you can't stop obsessing about, wondering how she got that

movie deal or television show, hit the *New York Times* best-sellers list for the tenth time in a row, or is now rich from a book you didn't even think was that good, do something nice. Congratulate her on Facebook. E-mail her. Buy her book. Celebrate her success. Praise her to one of your friends. You will be surprised how such an action drains the poison from your feelings. Fake it till you make it.

This approach has allowed me to become a real friend to the same one I once envied. Also, remember that this person is human, too. We only know the story everyone is talking about, not what really happened. Like that perfect marriage that breeds discontent behind closed doors, we cannot imagine what that author went through or is still going through. It may be all wine and roses on social media, but it may be stress, angst, confusion, and fear in real life.

It's not always all good.

When I begin to stray off course, looking over my shoulder or comparing my career to another, I remind myself one Holy Grail of truth.

There will always be someone more successful than you. Always.

There will always be someone less successful than you. Always.

I like this quote from Carrie Ann Ryan, reminding us to focus on our own journey:

> Head down, but not out. I'm constantly aware of changes in the market, promotion, craft, books I want to read, books *others* want to read, but I try not to let it overwhelm me. I can't write the next book and be who I need to be without keeping my head down at the same time. My head is down, writing what I love and knowing that while I need to pay attention to the market, it's not the only thing. I need to enjoy what I write and I also need to remember it's a business. It's a balance between the two, but being envious of another because my head isn't down and on my own projects isn't the answer.

Spending too much time obsessing with others' good or bad fortune takes energy from the writing. With every book you write, you have the chance for success. If you don't write anything, you will never have an opportunity to succeed.

When my book *The Marriage Bargain* hit the best-seller lists and my career exploded, I truly appreciated what that author had gone through. I hadn't counted on the many bad things to be twisted in with the good.

I hadn't realized I'd be called a fleeting, overnight success when I'd been writing regularly for twenty years, trying to make a living. I watched while others around me scrambled, judged, or stood beside me with strong support.

I'll tell you this: If those people who had my back felt any envy or jealousy, I didn't care. Their actions of kindness and support were all that truly mattered. And if they reached out to me even while they were jealous of my success, I understand, and I would have thanked them if I knew.

Actions do speak louder than words. Or feelings.

I still get jealous. And envious. But I'm more in tune with my limitations now, and I know when I'm looking outward instead of at my newest project. In other words, I have better coping skills now. I also take the time to close my eyes when I'm feeling rotten and to say a quick thank-you for what I do have. But if you receive an e-mail from me, praising your writing skills and congratulating you on hitting a list, please don't think that I'm secretly seething with jealousy.

These days I don't have to fake it as much, because my practices helped me find balance. I have realized that I am my own worst enemy. It was once easy to turn someone else's success into my own personal failure. I can recognize this tendency more accurately and stop the spiral before it takes hold.

I find when I'm feeling a bit raw, or struggling, I remove myself from social media for a while. Just to take a breath. How many times have you struggled with your word count, figured out you're probably getting dropped from your publisher, or checked your Amazon stats to see your sales tanked? Then you open up Facebook or Twitter and see this status everywhere:

> I just wrote 7K today! #amwriting

> Woot! Finished my book and signed a new 3 book contract!

> Thank you to all my readers for keeping my book on the best-seller list for 5 weeks! #readersrock

Yes, great stuff. Most of the time, you celebrate with them. Occasionally, when you are struggling with self-doubts, don't be afraid to turn off the computer and come back when you feel a bit stronger.

Writers are such sensitive creatures. We grow skin like rhinos to cope with the world, but inside we remain a mushy mess. We crave acceptance and love for our work. Is that so wrong? To want to share something beautiful with the world? Why should we torture ourselves for wanting to give back, for wanting to practice a creative art that makes sense of our lives?

Why is it so easy to remember the one crappy review and forget the multiple reviews praising our skill and thanking us for the book?

We're going to have to deal with jealousy at all stages of our careers. When we're not published, we're jealous of the published. When we're not signing big contracts, we're jealous of those seven-figure deals. When we don't hit the best-seller lists, we're jealous of those who do. It's an endless, vicious cycle. Break it by practicing kindness. Doing so allows your heart to catch up until you realize you're not really faking it anymore.

Somehow, along the way, the goodwill and acceptance become real.

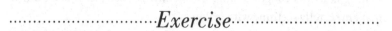

·····························*Exercise*·····························

Take a few minutes to go over your writing journey and your accomplishments. It doesn't matter if you're at the beginning or the peak of your career. Every word written, every rejection received, every book published means something, because it was a step forward that celebrated your creativity. Take the mental journey and then thank yourself for your bravery. Sometimes we turn our jealousy inward and brutalize our fragile psyche. This is a time to celebrate your accomplishments, not your failures. Write down the things you are most proud of. When you feel like crap, take out the list and remind yourself of how brave you truly are.

···

5

the write path

"*No trumpets sound when the important decisions of our life are made. Destiny is made known silently.*"

—AGNES DE MILLE

I never get tired of listening to a writer's journey.

At many of the Romance Writers of America conferences I attend, the keynote speakers are multipublished, best-selling authors. My favorite talks are the authors who detail their personal writing path, sharing what they learned along the way, their philosophies, and advice. I always leave feeling completely inspired and hopeful. Each of them faced many challenges—which is easy to identify with—and helps me believe I can one day reach the same level of success.

This is my journey and my lessons for you.

You can skip to the end of this chapter if you get bored. I promise this chapter is not just an ego trip down memory lane so I can gleefully expound on my success. I've had too many failures along the way to get cocky, and I've learned some things that I think you will find worthwhile. I also know my path will be completely different from yours. The publishing landscape has changed, but I still believe you'll be able to relate to the obstacles I encountered.

DREAMY BEGINNINGS

Simply put, I was born to write. I never had to search to find the career I wanted, because I knew in my bones I was meant to be a writer. What I recognized early on was the difficulty of making writing a full-time, *paying* job to support myself.

I wrote my first book at twelve years old, and spent the next years holed up in my room, writing three more back-to-back. I was a misfit. I didn't date. I was socially awkward. Thank goodness I had a group of friends who supported me and are still my best friends thirty years later. I got lucky. I was under the radar in school—not isolated enough to be bullied, but not interesting enough to be noticed. It was exactly where I wanted to be.

I entered a young adult writing contest, received my first rejection, and only became more motivated. Something told me that I was a real writer if I was writing. Being rejected meant I finished something and was gutsy enough to send it out. Writing after rejection meant I was fated to succeed, just because most aren't brave enough to continue after being told no.

First Challenges

I made my first mistake because I didn't know enough about the industry. I received a rejection letter from an agent I queried who told me my book had great potential but needed some work. She referred me to a manuscript-editing agency and said if I submitted to them, she'd take another look at my book.

I swiftly contacted the manuscript-editing agency. It would cost $500 for them to analyze the book. Back then, it might as well be $10,000, but I had been saving and decided to use my Christmas bonus toward the fee. I sent in the book and waited three months for feedback.

Finally, a letter came in the mail. It was three pages long. It detailed the summary of my manuscript, praised the characters, and gave me three suggestions. I had used "honey-colored" too much. My hero was a bit too alpha. And I had used "the fact is" five times too many.

That was it. Five hundred dollars later. Instead of getting nervous, I was weak with joy. I could fix those! And I'd resend to the agent, sign a contract, and be like a real writer!

write naked

I fixed the manuscript and resubmitted with the feedback from the agency. And was promptly rejected again.

·················*Lessons Learned*·················

Never pay for feedback, a critique, or anything that seems fishy. I went on to discover the wonderful Romance Writers of America and joined my local Hudson Valley RWA chapter. These women welcomed me with enthusiasm, gave me critique, feedback, and support. For free. They made me believe anything was possible, and I realized finding a community is absolutely critical for a writer. This is how we learn, how we share ideas, get opinions, and brainstorm. Yes, the writing is done alone, but we need to make sure we join others from our tribe. My tribe reminded me that I'm not clinically insane. I'm just another writer.

Secondary Challenges

I went on to pen my second adult romance at twenty-three and submitted it to Harlequin. They were interested. I sent them the manuscript with dreams of glory playing in my head, but didn't hear a peep for an entire year. When I finally summoned the courage to contact them—which I had been told to never, ever do—I learned the interested editor had left and they were sorry for the delay.

Three days later, I received a rejection from the new editor.

At this time, I wrote my third book and sent it through the rounds. I left no stone unturned. I also submitted articles and short stories to magazines, but couldn't seem to break in. So I continued my daily grind working in insurance, because it was the only way to pay my rent. I wrote evenings and weekends nonstop.

Finally, I submitted my eventual first book to an unknown publisher, LionHearted. Some authors warned me about them, but I sent it anyway. The editor actually called me and said they were interested. As I tried not to have a heart attack on the phone, I listened to her chatter nonstop for over an hour, learning I had to make some changes before she'd consider publishing it. The main one was to add a villain.

Umm, okay? It was a straight contemporary romance, no suspense, but if she wanted a villain, I'd give her one.

I rewrote the whole book and added in a lawyer.

Smart move, right?

She called me back and offered me a contract. A real, live contract. I was twenty-eight-years-old and had finally sold my first book.

I will never be able to properly describe how it feels to learn you have almost reached your dream. When I told my family, they were stunned. They were always supportive, but I knew they never expected me to actually publish a book. They figured I'd eventually grow tired and open up my own insurance agency. Suddenly, they looked at me with respect. I was barraged with questions. My phone rang off the hook. People couldn't believe I had finally signed a contract.

It was a great time in my life. I received the contract and looked it over carefully.

There was no set date for the book to be published. There was no guaranteed advance. There was no real set royalty payout schedule.

I signed it anyway.

That was my second mistake. I signed a *bad* contract.

I kept writing, and waited for my book to be published. And waited. And waited some more. My fervor diminished and I began avoiding social gatherings where endless people asked, "So when is this so-called book actually going to be published?"

Four years later, my book was published.

Let me repeat that. *Four years later, my book was published.*

Yeah, it was still great. The books came in a big box and I held them to my chest, kissed the cover, and slept with one that night. The partying began again, the calls started, the excitement, and I waited for the sales to begin racking up.

But it wasn't in bookstores. And books sold online fifteen years ago just weren't that popular.

I sold fifty copies. Mostly to friends, family, and one stranger in a clothes store because she felt pressured and I had a copy with me.

I earned one hundred dollars.

I never sold another copy. A few years later, the company went bankrupt.

Meanwhile, life marched past and a new genre exploded into the market—erotic romance. Publishers like Kensington and Red Sage took over, crafting beautiful covers to be displayed in bookstores. I became addicted. I always loved writing a good sex scene, and my work always received feedback of a scorching heat level. It was like I was born to write in this genre.

I penned a romance novella about a secret masquerade ball and submitted to Red Sage. They published it.

My mother was hardly thrilled, and she had to explain my latest story to the family—who is Italian Catholic—but that didn't diminish my joy of accomplishment. The story was packaged in an anthology with three other authors and issued in paperback format. It sold well, and they invited me to write another story for them. When I cashed my check for $3,000 I felt richer than Warren Buffett.

I worked on another erotic novella, but at this time, I also started writing a brand-new contemporary romance I titled, *The Marriage Bargain*. I was regularly submitting to Harlequin—still the big romance publisher in town—and receiving wonderful rejections. I felt like I was hovering, ready to begin steadily publishing, but was caught in this midlevel world where I couldn't seem to break through.

A small publishing company in California contacted me about my digital rights to my first book. They said they received the author list from LionHearted and were republishing all their defunct authors. They sent me a standard contract that was pretty bad. I was so depressed at the time, I signed it, knowing nothing was going to happen with that book anyway, especially in digital.

My third mistake was the same as my second. I signed *another* bad contract.

···················*Lessons Learned*···················

For God's sakes, don't sign a bad contract. In the current marketplace, contracts that tie up your rights need to be carefully vetted. Look carefully at the publisher's reputation, booklist, and financials. Look at the reversion clauses.

Look at the royalty structure and delivery dates. If you don't have an agent, ask around. Hire a literary lawyer to just look at the contract. Or contact the Author's Guild. Don't sign out of zeal and joy of having someone tell you your work is meaningful.

In the age of self-publishing, writers are being taken advantage of less often, but it's still a good warning to heed. I've read multiple blog posts with fabulous information on noncompete clauses and what *not* to sign. Treat your rights like the bounty treasure they are, and do not give them away without understanding every single clause and what it means.

....

THE MIDDLE YEARS

Life hit *hard*, mostly in good ways. I met my husband, got pregnant, married, bought a house, and rescued a dog. All in twelve months.

I changed jobs and commuted daily for an hour and a half, one way. I was thrust into the chaos of domestic life, with barely enough time to breath, let alone write. I had the baby, got pregnant again, rescued another dog, and began working on my master's degree in English Literature with the goal of becoming an English or creative writing professor. Writing was not paying the bills. I had little time on my hands, and I was completely overwhelmed. The next few years were a complete blur.

At this time, the Internet exploded. Blogging became huge. So did digital books. While working on literary essays and research papers, three other authors and I began a mommy blog—The Four Bad Mommies. It seemed the only thing I could write about was my children and diapers and poop and Baby Einstein.

Writing novels faded into the background. Being a mother became more important, emerging from the person I was before. It's hard to describe how motherhood changed me, but as I struggled, my lifeline became writing blogs. I wrote about the ups and downs. I wrote funny and sarcastic stories, as well as my daily search for the woman I'd left behind. I built a wonderful, solid following in the motherhood community. And that helped me. My essays kept my writing sharp, and I began journaling again, a practice that always tethered me to Earth when I felt overwhelmed by depression.

write naked

I graduated from college with my master's degree while my kids graduated from diapers. I realized I had to get back to my book, which I'd written a few years back, *The Marriage Bargain*. I edited, revised, and submitted again to the big publishers.

And I also decided to try my hand at another erotic novella. Three chapters in, I completely stalled out. Every time I sat down, my mind froze and I couldn't move forward with the story. I was frustrated. When I wasn't writing, I felt like I'd lost a part of myself I'd never replace. Writing was the essence of what made me who I was.

I spoke with my husband and asked if I could attend the National RWA conference that year. We had been saving for a new kitchen floor. He agreed that I needed to do something to get myself back on track and told me to go to the conference.

It was a turning point for me.

The conference was held in Orlando, Florida. I ended up meeting two writers who are now my very best friends in the community. I refilled my empty, sad well, which had been calling for me to write again. My creativity and enthusiasm exploded. I spoke with publishers and authors and took endless workshops. And one thing resonated with me over and over.

If I wanted to be a writer, I had to stop treating it like a hobby. I needed to treat it like a career. A serious career.

I returned home with a new motto and a clear focus. I made up a calendar and booked certain evenings where I would write and my husband would take care of dinner and the kids. I began plotting where I could find more time. I decided to dedicate my lunch hour for writing. I brainstormed during my commute. I went back into my office to my unfinished manuscript, deleted an entire chapter, and just started writing.

I had no more time for writer's block. I was on a mission.

THE SEEDS OF SUCCESS

Already familiar with running a blog, I created my own website and used my contacts to build a following. I only had one published novella, and *Heart of Steel* originally with LionHearted, but I swore I'd be ready when publishers came calling.

I sold my new erotic novella to Red Sage Publishing. They agreed to publish it digitally. Upon signing the contract, I learned they wanted more from me, so I began on a second erotic novella.

I met with some fellow authors from the conference who had published successfully with another small company, Decadent Publishing. They had a line of short (15,000-word) erotic stories revolving around the concept of a one-night stand. I seemed to be doing quite well in the short erotic category, so I penned a quick story and submitted it to the editor. She contacted me a few hours later. She loved it and agreed to publish it. Then she asked me if I was interested in writing two additional short stories to create a series. I agreed, and sold them both.

I'd built my foundation. In the upcoming year, four works would be published. I had a website, good relationships with reviewers, and solid contacts with bloggers.

And during the conference, I'd learned about a new digital publishing company, Entangled. I thought I'd try one last time to submit *The Marriage Bargain*, which had been rejected almost twenty times by every big- and small-name publisher. I stubbornly kept at it. This book was special. I felt like it had a magic I couldn't explain, and I was desperate to get it into the hands of readers.

This was 2011. Self-publishing was just beginning to rise in popularity and some self-published authors were becoming well-known. But I didn't quite feel ready to dive into those waters with this book. I wanted the backing of a publishing company.

Now, at this time, my boss—a horrible man—was torturing me at my day job. He verbally abused me and sent me home crying every day. I couldn't quit though, because we had bills to pay. Eventually, though, they laid me off.

Unemployment for a mom with two young kids is a bitch. I had a master's degree, endless experience, excellent referrals, and I couldn't find a damn job. So I got creative and did anything possible to make money. I sold lia sophia jewelry. I worked at my friend's diner and made Rachel from *Friends* seem like an awesome waitress. I freelanced for editors. I tried teaching online. It was a scary time, but as I tirelessly searched for employment, I also wrote like a fiend.

I submitted *The Marriage Bargain* to Entangled. I received an e-mail back from the editor, who quickly scheduled a call with me. They wanted to buy the book and publish it on Valentine's Day in 2012. They had a unique vision to compete with Harlequin on a digital scale and they wanted fresh, unique romance books. Their plan was to price them at $2.99 and release four per month.

It was a brilliant, unique idea, and I was on board. My book would be part of the launch.

The week my book launched, my unemployment was running out. At this point, I rarely slept, worried about my family's future. I begged for a sign. I prayed and asked to be shown the way. At this point, as much as I loved writing, I'd have taken any job or done anything to keep my family afloat. I was terrified that we'd lose our house because we just couldn't support ourselves on one income.

My book released. It was an exciting day to see the novel I'd written five years ago land in the hands of readers. Now, at this time, my boys had traded one of those wicked stomach viruses and I fell victim to it that evening. For twenty-four hours I was pinned to the bathroom floor, and then spent the following twenty-four hours recovering in bed. Two days later, I emerged from my cave, blinking and feeling like I'd been run over by a Mack Truck.

I went to my computer and checked my e-mail ...

And learned that everything had exploded into chaos.

My book had reached the number one spot on the Barnes & Noble website. *The Hunger Games* was number two.

I called my husband over and told him the computer was broken. We powered it down, restarted, went back to the site, and saw the same thing. The phone began ringing. It was the most awe-inspiring, amazing feeling of my life. I laughed, cried, and screamed with my editors.

A week or two later, the book hit the top spot on Amazon, too. I'll never forget the night I returned home from dinner with friends and my husband launched himself across the room, screaming for me to call my editor. When I did, I learned *The Marriage Bargain* had hit the *USA Today* best-seller list. One week later, it hit the *New York Times*.

We were awestruck.

Perhaps even more baffling was how this little romance novel stormed the charts and didn't budge. We never expected it to hit an actual bestseller list, because this had never been done before. It was *digital*, after all. No one had ever heard of me. How had this happened?

It was the perfect storm, I think. You start with a great book, but the rest is a mix of luck, work, placement, faith, fate, and more work. It was the right price and the right idea at the right time. I'd released three other books back-to-back-to-back in a short amount of time, so reviewers were buzzing and promo was busily churning—it seemed natural to keep press and reviews churning for this book. *Fifty Shades of Grey* had hit epic proportions and readers flocked to *The Marriage Bargain* next. Multiple readers informed me *The Marriage Bargain* was the second book they read after *Fifty Shades of Grey*, and recommended it to all of their friends. The stars aligned perfectly, and I got swept up in the moment.

As the book stuck to the lists and refused to budge, the calls began to come. Agents. Publishers. Authors. At this point, I had no agent or other representation. Now, as publication offers poured in from every corner of the country, I needed some help.

I signed with an agent. Months passed, the book still sold like the next hot thing, and New York publishers approached us with interest in buying out the series. It was like a Lifetime movie of the week and I was the star. After being rejected by everyone, this book was now a must-have for every publisher.

Life has always been stranger than fiction.

THE BIG TIME

Now, let me explain the difference between this book and other self-published authors who skyrocketed at this time. I only owned fifty percent of the book. Entangled Publishing owned the other half. My contract said the publisher could sell out, but as an individual, I could not. At this point, I wasn't looking to leave Entangled or move on to a new publisher, but Entangled agreed I should meet with all the publishers in New York and give Entangled feedback. Entangled and I worked as a team and tried to come to a consensus for our final decision.

I listened to the New York publishers' pitches and reported back. We teetered between letting the series go to auction and keeping it with Entangled. The main problem revolved around paperback issue. Since Entangled was strictly a digital publisher at that time, getting the book distributed in stores in mass paperback was an obstacle. Entangled made some contacts and found a distributer that was willing to get the books in stores. But it was a game of roulette. If the book sold well and went immediately to a second printing, Entangled may not have enough money to allow a second printing. But the book could also tank and we'd be out tons of money. Giving it over to an established New York publisher seemed to be the best bet, but I was still willing to gamble. Sure, I was entranced with heading over to the Big 5 (at the time), but I also felt loyalty toward Entangled, since they were the ones to take the chance on my book.

On my agent's advice, Entangled and I decided to go to auction. When the final number rolled in, it was seven figures. We rejected the offer and decided to allow Entangled to publish the book on its own.

Between frantic calls, upset agents, and mass confusion, I wrote the second book of the series, placing my head in a vise full of pressure. I needed it to be as good as the first because everyone was counting on me, but we were still dealing with important decisions regarding *The Marriage Bargain*.

Everyone seemed to have a different opinion on the best route for the book. Relationships became strained. Eventually, *The Marriage Bargain* went to a second auction and Simon & Schuster won, along with the second and third book in the series.

I can only try to explain how this hurricane of events affected me while I spoke at writing conferences, toiled on the third book in the series, and pretended everything was perfect. *The Marriage Bargain* had now spent twenty-seven weeks on the *New York Times* best-seller list. Simon & Schuster distributed the book everywhere. I met with my new editor, who'd work with me on the final book in the series.

As soon as the book published, it reflected the new digital price of $7.99.

The book immediately dropped off the *New York Times* list and never made its way back.

Yes, success is very, very sweet. I remember an article detailing the top five books left behind in hotel rooms around the country. *Fifty Shades of Grey* was number one.

The Marriage Bargain was number two.

···················*Lessons Learned*····················

Don't undervalue yourself. We want people to love us. We desire validation. But sometimes certain offers are too good to be true. Don't let the excitement of success lure you to make impulsive decisions. Look at all your options before deciding. Be brave and think big. If you value yourself and your work, you won't get caught short.

THE FALLOUT

I wonder if anyone is truly prepared for the chaos that can sometimes come with success. I think you need to be strong within yourself and attempt to suppress your ego. You need to remember that the fanfare will eventually die, someone else will grab the spotlight, and you will have only the memories. But you'll have *your* books. The focus needs to remain on writing, and writing your best story, or you will lose your way.

By fall, I had two lawyers, an accountant, an assistant, and a new agent. Rumors circulated about my breakup with Entangled and heading to Simon & Schuster without a look back. People who wouldn't give me the time of day suddenly wanted to be my best friend. I was asked for endless blurbs. I had to be careful of what I said, who I trusted, and how everyone perceived me.

I'd like to quickly go back to remind you of that last bad contract I signed for my first book, *Heart of Steel*. Remember that? The one that was published in digital format, that I figured nothing would ever happen with, and that I just forgot about?

Well, when readers discovered *Bargain*, they quickly foraged my backlist. There wasn't much there, other than *Heart of Steel*. It shot up the charts and made a lot of money. When I initially tried to contact my publisher regarding the book, I was ignored. They never called back. They swept it under the carpet.

But now, this small publisher was shocked at the profit rolling in. They decided to put the book in print, dump money into editing, secure a new cover, and begin actual promotion. The publisher enlisted my help, and I spent a few months revising the book, approving covers, edits, and marketing materials.

After endless effort, correspondence, and phone calls, they published my book in print. Then they pulled it and decided to do a different cover. They went through three editors. It was a mess that I should've been wary about, but I had signed the contract without doing my research.

The publisher owed me over $50,000 by the time royalties were due. I received $2,000. Then $3,000.

Then, nothing.

The publisher dodged my phone calls and whined about income flow to his company. Getting nervous over the huge amount of money I was owed, counted on, and wasn't receiving, I hired a lawyer. I'll spare you the details. After a year of legal work, I didn't see another dime. The publisher ran off and claimed bankruptcy.

Goodbye $50,000.

Hello, valuable lesson.

By the time all three of my books in the Marriage to a Billionaire series were published, I'd completed my own growth arc. I'd been involved with two lawsuits, hired a team of people to help me, began speaking engagements (which is my number one all time fear—worse than spiders), and written several more books. I had my trust completely broken, but I dealt with it and put myself back together. I became stronger.

······················*Lessons Learned*······················

People will break your heart when you achieve success. It's human nature. I'm not trying to be a negative Nelly, but I've seen the greed firsthand. The viciousness of social media tearing apart successful authors or planting bad reviews is part of this world. The way to combat all of this is stay true to yourself. You won't have any regrets if your intentions are good, and you do your best to avoid hurting anyone. I lost a lot of money, opportunities, and sleep along the way, but I don't regret any of it, because it taught me to hang in and not to compromise.

People will heal your heart when you achieve success. There are so many authors and friends who stood by me—no questions asked—even when rumors flew. They believed in me. The people who should be in your life for the long-term will stand by you. The people who don't were only meant to visit for a short time.

....

THE GOOD, THE BAD, AND THE WORK

Once I reached that shattering pinnacle of success, my other demons appeared. The market began to change. Many readers didn't want to pay more for my e-book than they had in the past. I was new to the print market and trying to earn a good reputation with readers who had no experience with digital. I'd received a hefty advance along with enormous expectations of what I should sell and produce.

Let's just say that combination wasn't too great for my temperamental, cranky muse.

She disappeared. I'd signed a nice, fat three-book contract and began the first book in a new series. The months that followed featured a lot of crying to my husband and kids, who didn't really understand what was going on. I was paralyzed with fear and decided if I didn't hit the bestseller list, it was all over. My career would be over.

Writing that book was painful—for everyone. My editor coached me through it, and the only way the story emerged was by developing blisters on my ass from sitting for hours. Not writing. Just staring. And worrying. And cursing.

I embraced the pain, gritted my teeth, and eventually I wrote that book. I still hold very strong emotions for *Searching for Someday*. It reminds me of when my second son's birthday comes around. He gave me a hard time during labor, as I reached pinnacles of pain that shouldn't exist. At one point, I'd leapt from the bed and put my husband in a chokehold, telling him in a vicious whisper to get the drugs *now*. Today I look at that kid with such pride, joy, and love, but on his birthday, I wince a bit at the memory of that pain.

Someday was this book for me.

The book hit the *USA Today* list but not the *Times*. I went to bed and admitted to myself I'd failed. Yeah, I know, the unpublished writers are now throwing this book at a wall and cursing me. The published writers who experienced this are nodding their heads with complete understanding.

See, the game had changed for me from writing a great book to *selling* a book. Once your mind makes that change, writing becomes different. It's like getting into bed and having the entire neighborhood with you, throwing out comments and the occasional insult while you wonder what they're doing there.

I became crippled by the idea that I'd let important people down. People who believed in me. My publisher, my editor, agent, reviewers, and readers. They were all in the bed with me, and you can't write your best when you've got an audience.

The second book in my series, *Searching for Perfect*, tanked. I believe it was one of my best books, and readers seemed to embrace and adore it. But the sales just weren't there.

At this time, my publisher decided we'd made a grievous error in branding the covers. As much as I loved the art, nothing told the reader it was a spin-off from the popular Marriage to a Billionaire series. They didn't seem to fit anywhere and didn't pop on the shelves. My publisher was savvy enough not to give up on me, redesigning the covers for the next books, which sold better and garnered some of my highest and critically acclaimed reviews.

But they still didn't hit the *Times*. And I had to live with it.

I wonder if writers who have penned over a hundred books still feel unbalanced, and afraid of letting their team down, when they sit down to write. I bet they do. The beauty of self-publishing is the knowledge that if my book doesn't sell, I've only let myself down. I can live with that so much easier. It gives me a chance to take a breath and experiment, because I don't have an advance or expectations to worry about—it's just me and my readers.

Of course, when you're full-time indie, there's no advance, so you do worry about sales because it may make the difference between eating and not eating. No matter what kind of writer you are—traditional, indie, or hybrid—there are always concerns.

When I think of how ridiculous hitting a *New York Times* list sounds as a component for failure, I'm embarrassed. There was a time in my life where I just craved having an audience. Or a single reader. So I consistently remind myself not to get so caught up in the writing business that I lose sight of the power of the product.

There is a wonderful teen movie called *Center Stage*. It's about a group of ballerinas studying together, hoping to make it big. One of the ballerinas is a real badass—she's talented, but her fear and inner demons seem to come out at the wrong times. In one scene, the teacher finds her practicing ballet alone, and her raw talent and beautiful dance stuns the teacher. She walks over to the ballerina and tells her that life is a mess, obstacles are everywhere, and we are all searching for something. Something important. Something that makes sense. Something that feeds our soul and soothes our heart.

"It's not out there," she says softly. Then she touches the ballet barre. "It's here."

See, when things don't make sense, go back to the barre.

The barre, guys. Not the bar.

When you get too confused over your writing career, go back to the page. That's where the answers will always be.

······························*Exercise*··························

Think about a time in your life when writing was really hard. Did you think about quitting? Changing careers? How did you manage to keep going? Connect with a personal moment when you doubted your writing. Examine where you are now, and where you want to be. What actions can you take to keep writing? What fills up and empties your creative well? Target one positive change you can institute in your writing life to help you write, or lessen your doubts. Commit to that change.

write naked

6

the "real" writer

"Our lives are at once ordinary and mythical. We live and die, age beautifully or full of wrinkles. We wake in the morning, buy yellow cheese, and hope we have enough money to pay for it. At the same instant we have these magnificent hearts that pump through all sorrow and all winters we are alive on the earth. We are important and our lives are important, magnificent really, and their details are worthy to be recorded. This is how writers must think, this is how we must sit down with pen in hand. We were here; we are human beings; this is how we lived. Let it be known, the earth passed before us. Our details are important. Otherwise, if they are not, we can drop a bomb and it doesn't matter."

—NATALIE GOLDBERG, *WRITING DOWN THE BONES*

When people ask me who I am, I always answer instinctively, "A writer."

Not a mom. Not a woman. Not a wife. Not a friend. A writer. Being a writer defines the essence of who I am—and sometimes that's scary. At times in my life, I've found myself shaking with the need to compose, to scribble down thoughts, to calm the demons. It's how I make sense of this world and all its raw, naked, brutal glory.

It is not an easy life. Being an artist never is. But writers can find a greater payback than other occupations, and I think that's what consistently drives us forward.

Since I was young, I ached to be a real writer. To me, that meant publication and readers other than my mother. It meant I'd finally be able to share my viewpoint and philosophy with the world and see if I made a small difference. Each committed word changed me and helped me grow. As I aged, the writing changed. As I gained more experience in life and love and heartbreak, the writing became richer, like perfectly tilled soil, prepped to accept the roots of a plant.

I found solace in stories about love, first kisses, and growing up. They buzzed with the passion and the messiness of youth—full of angst and hormones desperately screaming for an outlet. Writing young adult romance helped me imagine myself in that world I craved. And since I created it, I could be the reigning star.

One weekend my cousins visited and discovered my full manuscript stuffed in my desk drawer. My cousin pulled it out, her mouth open like a guppy, and asked what it was. Feeling horribly uncomfortable and embarrassed, I squirmed and told her I wrote a book. She blinked, focused on me, and shook her head. Then said, "You don't date much, do you?"

I was humiliated. She was right. I was way behind on experiences like boyfriends, proms, and social cliques. I was too busy trying to find myself by writing. I later realized writing saved me, but at the time, I wished I was a different type of person. I felt weird. I didn't know anyone else like me. Today, there's much more support for young writers, especially online, but I still believe artists will always struggle with the feeling they are separate from other people. I never quite belonged anywhere, because a part of me was studying and furiously creating mental notes during every conversation, lecture, and commute. I imagine if aliens ever invaded Earth, the artists would be the first to welcome and understand them.

When I was a college student, I craved to explore the lofty philosophies of famous artists, and immerse myself in poetry and texts seeping with hidden meaning.

As I grew, sex became more important, along with the quest for a deeper type of long-term relationship. Writing adult contemporary romance was a perfect fit. I enjoyed writing erotic sex scenes, and exploring the connection between a man and woman forging careers and living full, fabulous lives. I also tried to figure out where my life was going, which led me to a decade of intense yoga and meditation practices. At one point, I found myself cross-legged in an Ashram, chanting and searching for inner peace and calm. I dove into writing about yoga, spirituality, and transcending body into spirit. I turned vegetarian and became a yoga instructor. It was a critical point in my life that helped me connect with who I was as a writer.

When I became a mother, I obsessed over stories depicting the ups and downs of motherhood. I needed humor to get through the smell of poop and the constant exhaustion and confusion. I wanted to connect with who I was before motherhood.

We must understand that our experiences consistently change us as people and writers. Writing is an energy that is alive and flowing in ebbs and tides. What we believed in yesterday may change tomorrow. In this way, we are re-creating our lives, our outlook, and the words we commit to the page. There is also a struggle to redefine our writing paths, and we must try to understand not only what we need as writers, but also what we need to live happily in our day-to-day routine.

When I moved from part-time writer to full-time, I faced many obstacles I never imagined.

Before *The Marriage Bargain* became big, I'd published one book and six novellas. After *The Marriage Bargain*, I published nineteen more stories within four years. I dedicated myself to growing my backlist and taking advantage of this once-in-a-lifetime opportunity of interested readers. Of course, I was able to write full-time, so that helped, but I also committed to my writing—and to myself. I wanted to write every day.

But the move to writing full-time was a struggle. For years, I'd lived my life snatching time here and there to write. I sacrificed social events, television, books, and family time in my quest to get words on the paper. My writing time was sacred.

Suddenly, I had massive amounts of free time during the day to write. My children were in school. My husband was at work. The dogs slept all day. Nothing would distract me from my pursuit of heavy word counts. In pure amazement, I calculated the amount of words I'd write, and how easily I could make my deadlines. This was too easy!

And then things got in the way. Weird things. I'd always proudly told people I didn't do a lot of cleaning. I wasn't the domesticated sort, despised cleaning at all costs, and adhered to a philosophy that told me if it was only going to get dirty again soon, why bother in the first place? I'd let stuff pile up, not worry about the little things, and hired a cleaner to come in every other week for the deep scrubbing.

Imagine my shock when that first week passed in a blur of ... cleaning. I'd sit with my coffee, respond to e-mail, update social media, waste time on the Internet, then take a deep breath and open up my manuscript.

Until I found the need to wash my coffee cups. And let the dogs out one more time. And notice my laundry needed sorting. I was home now. I needed to do a bit more of my share because I had all this extra time to write. After all, I'd already squeezed out a book while scraping for writing time. Now, I'd be able to take care of the house, help my husband, *and* write a lot.

My family seemed to agree. My husband began calling me from work with a list of errands. I found myself grocery shopping, dealing with the gas company, calling the cable company, taking the car in for an oil change, and a dozen other details I'd never deign to do in the past. Friends who had toddlers at home began to call, asking if I could watch their child for just an hour. My phone rang off the hook. My mother grumbled and griped when I declined lunch, telling me I was home now, and I certainly had the time.

I found, at the end of thirty days, I had almost no new writing. Nada. I muttered under my breath about my husband not helping and found myself caught up in a cycle of resentment while my deadline ticked away. How had this happened?

Somehow I had lost my way due to my interpretation of time. I began to devalue the importance of my work. Instead of greedily protecting my writing time, I tossed the minutes away as if there was an endless surplus in the day. I treated my writing like it was disposable, so no new words appeared on the page.

My mind couldn't make sense of what happened, and I decided to reevaluate. It took almost another month to grow strong enough to create boundaries in my life. In a way, I started from square one when I began writing full-time. I had to stand up and announce I was a writer and that my time at home was sacred. I had a long talk with my husband, explained my frustrations, and he understood. I learned to say no. A lot. Much more than I was comfortable with as a huge people pleaser. But slowly, I began to do the main thing that writers need in order to succeed.

I protected the work.

Finally, I fell into a routine, discovering the schedule that worked best. Some writers go by daily word count. Some by time spent actually writing. You need to find what works best for you, whether it's an ambitious morning schedule and flexible afternoons, or vice versa. But you must treat your writing like a job. As Nora Roberts says, "I'm the hardest boss anyone could ever have."

Yet, writing is not like filing. We need to be our own taskmasters, but a creative profession must include room to breathe, change, and grow.

I spoke earlier about how writing for yourself is very different than writing for a publisher or a deadline. Expectations change everything. It's like there's a bigger chance of failure once you've been published. You have more to lose. You're no longer just writing. You're a business entity responsible for a website, promotion, marketing, and a product. The stakes climb very high.

After composing so many contemporary romance novels back to back, my muse began to get cranky. I craved something different. I wanted to stretch my writing muscles and fly.

Self-publishing was the key to my freedom. I was growing a brand with Simon & Schuster, which was extremely important. Vital, even. But I was also a creative person with a soul that longed to fly in new directions— I know myself very well. If I didn't give myself the room, I'd wither up and churn out bad writing. Again, my advice is to know yourself. Get to know your habits—good and bad—and what you need to stay fresh and grounded in your writing.

I'd spoken to an author at a writers conference and she broached the subject of doing a project together. Something different. The new adult market had exploded, and I was interested in trying my hand at a story. This had nothing to do with chasing the market. I'd had no desire to write new adult. I'd also steered away from writing first person, preferring third person. In fact, writing in first person scared me. But when we sketched out an idea for three books—all connected, but still stand-alone—about three college friends on spring break that find love, it felt fresh and fun.

And that, specifically, is why I signed on for the project.

Because it was self-published and I was writing with two friends, I had zero expectations. I wasn't doing it to hit a list, get rich, or impress anyone. I followed the story, experimented with voice, and had fun. Readers embraced the new direction and *Beyond Me* actually ended up hitting the *New York Times* best-seller list.

That was back in 2013, though. The market is completely different today—glutted, which makes it harder to get your book in front of bloggers and readers who have endless choices, many either free or available for ninety-nine cents.

I made a decision to price my self-published work in the average range. Novellas would cost $2.99. Full-length, $4.99. The prices were still cheaper than my traditional books, but allowed me some leeway to create sales.

My goal became simple: Write the bigger books with Simon & Schuster while publishing independently to build my backlist. The key with self-publishing is the rights. You own them. You say when, how much, how long, and you pick your content. It's a great way to experiment with different genres or to discover a new audience niche.

My main problem revolved around time. I wanted to focus on writing books and not become swamped in the details of launching a successful indie career. I decided to work with a publishing partner called Cool Gus Publishing. Our agreement was clear and simple: Cool Gus took care of all the mechanics in publishing the book, including editing, formatting, uploading to all platforms, cover design, and basic marketing. In return, they received a percentage of my royalties. They became trusted advisors while I retained control of my rights and what I wanted to write. They met with all publishing representatives from Amazon, Apple, Barnes & Noble,

Kobo, and Google Play. Cool Gus helped arrange sales and BookBub ads, analyzed my algorithms, and created video trailers and slide shares. They even issued a free book called, *Sneak Peeks*, which offered readers sample chapters of all my work and included exclusive behind-the-scenes content. Cool Gus and I still work together to continuously brainstorm about fresh ways to bring my work to new readers.

This type of partnership works well for me, and we have now issued eight books together, with an ambitious schedule for the upcoming year. But no matter how much help you have, certain books seem to do better than others for various reasons.

For example, after *Beyond Me*, I wrote the sequel *Chasing Me*, and the sales weren't that good. This fascinated me. The book featured the same characters, same genre, same type of covers, and was released around the same time. We followed the same exact marketing strategy, including the ninety-nine cent price point for only preorders, an extensive blog tour, social media advertising, and the combination of all our newsletter lists and street teams.

Yet, the sequel tanked.

Another lesson learned: You cannot repeat the same magic because the market is consistently changing. That's another reason this business is so hard. The moment you have things figured out, the market shifts, and you need a brand-new plan.

Still, I don't regret it. I felt the book was solid, I had fun, and I learned. I also now had a strong dual set, with the ability to offer the first book for free or discounted.

My other forays into genres include a paranormal novella based on superheroes. Inspired by my son's adoration of superheroes, which forced me to Google every character multiple times, I ached to write this one. I was an aficionado on the subject at that point and grew to truly respect the growth of superheroes and the tortured-hero type. My idea was for a trilogy of connected superheroes, so I wrote *Dante's Fire* and released it into the world.

It sold less than *Chasing Me*. Ouch.

I realized now that the cover wasn't the right fit, and I eventually updated the look for an uptick in sales. The second book scheduled was pushed back due to time constrictions with my Simon & Schuster contract, so I pushed the trilogy to the back of my mind. Eventually, I intend to finish the trilogy and promote it as a set.

I also decided to reissue three erotic novellas after I resecured my rights from the publisher. This included an extensive rewrite to update the stories, new covers, and a complete repackaging of the brand. I decided to write a fourth novella for readers who had already read the series, and issued them a week apart.

My vision for my career included consistent releases every few months in an effort to keep building my brand and reader base. My writing schedule was extremely ambitious, with both traditional and indie book releases. It revolved around working on a one-hundred-thousand-word book for a good three months, revising, copyediting, and diving into a self-published novella. At that time, I'd also need to promote the first book, and the cycle would repeat. Simply put, there were not enough hours in my day, especially when the new writing moved slower than I wanted.

As you know, I'm a big advocate of sitting in the chair and forcing out words, but I also know a good writing day can mean one decent page, and another day can mean two thousand words. When I hit the last quarter of a book, I clock in four- to five-thousand words every day.

Yet, each time I hit a new stage in the process, I still worry. I wonder if this is the last book I'll ever write. I worry my Muse permanently packs up for vacation in Vegas and decides to stay for good. I torture myself with comparisons to previous books, other author's books, and the horrific middle where I fall apart each and every time like clockwork.

If I've written over twenty-five books, why do I still worry? Why don't I ever confidently strut my stuff and act like a rock star?

Every time I open up a Word document, I start at square one. I sit and stare at the screen, gripped in terror that I have to do this all over again. Will it all fall apart this time? Will I finally reveal my big secret? That I'm just a big, fat fraud?

That's depressing.

And sometimes, exhausting.

Oh, and it's also imposter syndrome, which most successful women suffer from. I diagnosed myself with it at an early age. I was taking a psychology class in college and my professor wrote the term on the board. He explained that *imposter syndrome* occurs when no matter how successful a person is, whether she's winning trophies, getting As on tests, or writing and publishing books, she feels like a fraud. A person suffering from imposter syndrome convinces herself the teacher was easy on her, or that she finished too close to her opponent in the race to really deserve the trophy, or that her book succeeded because it had the right cover or blurb or that it really wasn't her talent, it was just … luck.

I remember blinking at the board, and the fog around me suddenly shriveled up, revealing the clear road ahead. *Yes!* I shouted to myself. *That's me! I finally found out what I have!*

The problem was how to fix it. There's no real cure. Just a lot of practice trying to believe in yourself, and repeating helpful tasks. Mine were journaling, meditating at an ashram, and seeking spiritual peace to transition my fears away from my work. Today, it's spending time with my boys, my dogs, and my family. Family time reminds me I have other important aspects of my life and helps me balance my vision of my work.

But there's always going to be fear and that's part of the package. We need to learn to live with it, and to coexist peacefully with it, and to accept with grace that it will always be our companion.

Fear can be a very valuable tool that helps push your career forward. I have learned one lesson that I share with all of my workshop students and writer friends: If something scares you, you should do it. You're scared for a reason. Fear is the slithering snake whispering vile things in your ear, making you think this new venture will be a total disaster. Usually, it won't be. If it is, it's still worth the risk, because you'll learn something.

Mistakes are good. You cannot do everything perfectly in this life, and I promise you, even after reading this book, listening to workshops, and taking advice from your mentors, you are going to make mistakes. You'll probably make a lot of them. Good for you. At least you're living, and if you're living, you have something great to write about.

Our lives become textures mingled into our writing, and the richer, the better. The page is a safe place to dive deep, to release the demons, and to unleash them on the world. It will be uncomfortable and sometimes painful. You will want to quit. But if you follow through, you may be surprised you've reached levels in your writing you've never achieved before.

Stake your claim in this world and show us what no one has before. There will be many people who won't understand or agree with your viewpoint. There will be many people who do, and who read your book and *feel* something.

Every good book I read changes me in some small way. It could be a simple scene, character, or the chemistry between hero and heroine. It could be the richness of setting, the title, or the cover. It could be that the book drew me in, and I forgot about real life for a little while. Those moments are precious.

We are the people who deliver those moments. Doesn't that make us a little bit immortal? Don't writers exhibit naked vulnerability and massive courage to put their work out there into the public hands? Don't writers risk everything, with the possibility of having their work literally and figuratively ripped apart, analyzed, and mocked, all in the quest for just one reader to fall in love?

Count me in. That's the type of career and life I want to live. I may be the shy, plain girl in the corner of a rollicking party, but on the page I am a tigress, a fire in the tundra, a glittering ruby buried in a pile of jagged slate rocks.

Katy Perry tells us to roar and light up like a firework. Rocky tells us it's not how many times you get hit, but how many times you get back up. Rachel Platten tells us it only takes a small spark to start a fiery explosion. Barry Manilow tells us to make our own parade (don't judge me people).

There will be many times in this career that you will have to make choices, and sometimes going the artistic route won't be feasible. Writers with strict contracts may find themselves locked in with a publisher and not able to self-publish for a while. Authors who juggle day jobs may not be able to write that extra book, choosing to spend their precious free time with family or developing promotions for their book.

I don't think there are wrong choices, but you must give each one careful consideration. If you are a writer, and you bought this book, you want to be a *career* writer. You want a body of work that grows along the way, and it just may grow slower and more organically than other authors.

I know, because I reached different stages of my career over the past thirty years. Looking back, I see how each stage fit to free me up for the next. At the time, I saw nothing but my bitter frustration of how my life was passing me by and I'd never "make it."

Success means different things to different people. My publishing partner, Cool Gus, consistently repeats the magic phrase to all authors: *There are many roads to Oz.*

I have that printed on my wall to help remind me I'm not other writers. I'm me. I have my own path, and I need to follow it with a truthful heart. I never could have sustained my current writing schedule when I had two kids in diapers. But, at that time, I followed a path that was right for me.

Be bold, but be patient. Don't ever expect to explode out of the gate. I always preferred betting on the long shot anyway—it was a much bigger payoff and a damn fun surprise.

Exercise

Write down what success means for you. Then write down your goal for one year and five years. Commit to paper the things you want to achieve and the small steps necessary to get there. It's amazing how good it feels to cross even one item off your list. Seeing career goals on paper changes things—it makes them possible. It makes them real.

7

commit to marriage;
avoid the affairs

"I went for years not finishing anything. Because, of course, when you finish something you can be judged."

—ERICA JONG

Some writers have commitment problems.

When I first started writing seriously, I chased ideas like a dog in heat. It was part of the learning phase, and I let myself experiment. I wrote short stories, blogs, articles, and essays. I wrote romance novels. Young adult. I wrote cards I thought I'd sell to Hallmark, and poetry that was so awful even my mother had to break the news to me.

Many projects were scattered around me, abandoned in notebooks, and filed away in folders full of Word documents. Eventually, though, I grew up and wanted to submit and publish my stories. I realized I needed to finish projects with regularity and spend time and effort caring for a story, rather than ditching it at the first sign of trouble.

Writers tell me all the time they don't need to finish a story or a piece. They enjoy writing what they want, when they want it, and if the interest is there, then they'll finish it. Or not. I know writers who wrote first books for a series and decided to never follow through with the rest of the series because another project caught their eye. I've seen writers announce that a new blog post will be available on a certain date, only to log on at that time to find their latest post was weeks ago. I've watched writers pitch a billion ideas with blurbs and outlines, and never deign to actually finish one story.

Personally, I think the failure to follow through is one of the biggest mistakes a writer can make. Sure, the new, exciting story in the forefront of your mind is shiny. It's bright and virginal and full of possibilities. You catch your wandering eye straying from your current manuscript, which, right now, is *not* pretty. Your current manuscript is familiar. It's boring. It's the DUFF—Designated Ugly Fat Friend—to the newfound, hot story that's brewing in your mind. It feels like you'll be stuck with the current story forever, and honestly, it's not what you initially signed up for. You thought this time would be different. This time, you'd love your current manuscript so damn much, no pretty little temptress would get the best of you.

Yet here she is. Strolling in with a naughty wink and endless pages of blinding white space. It'll be so much better if you make the leap and leave your current ball and chain. You can get out of it. It's not like you promised your soul to the devil on this one! No sir, this new book is going to be *the one*. You *swear*.

You jump. Maybe you're a quarter through your "old," current manuscript. Maybe even halfway—where the middle has been killing you, slowly and tortuously. Finally, with this new idea, you can breathe. The muse has sprung to life at the promise of a new story, proving you made the right decision.

You quickly dive in, maybe draft an outline or write a spectacular beginning. Chapter one is the best chapter you ever wrote in your life. The *best*. Disney birds are singing, and the glass slipper finally fits. Chapter two roars past, and you're still riding high. But by chapter four, uh, things have slowed.

You tell yourself not to worry. Maybe go back to the outline. Maybe if you dig a bit deeper you'll rediscover the magic. The dating. The sex. Oh, God, the sex! It can't be over so soon, can it? Can it?

This time, you don't even get to the middle before you falter. The words begin to trickle instead of flow. You lose your motivation, you hate your hero, and stupid things are happening for no reason. This book sucks. You should have stayed with the first one. You could have whipped it into shape, but now you're stuck. It's too far gone to go back to your original manuscript. You grit your teeth, swear you'll get through it no matter what, and then you catch a glimpse of something so shiny, you stumble and stop. It looks like diamonds and gold and pearls all blended together in a blinding, beautiful vision.

"What is this?" you ask. Slowly, you turn your head. And it's over. A new idea just tempted you once again, and the cycle continues.

For God's sake, guys, finish the damn book.

Sometimes marriage really sucks. You don't have sex nearly as much, and kids make you tired and cranky. You're done with romance, flowers, and surprises. Hell, if your spouse cooks dinner or does laundry you have an orgasm. But underneath the grit and daily grind of life, there's a love that keeps you going. You *get* each other. Yeah, it's hard, and some days are better than others, but occasionally you catch your spouse's eye, or share a laugh, or tease him in the only way he'd understand, and the magic is there. It's real magic, too, not fake. It's magic based on a hell of a lot of work overcoming failure, ups and downs, and respect.

Sign me up.

In the beginning, books are like affairs, because excitement drives you forward. But the deeper you get into the book, the more you discover hidden problems.

The conflict wasn't pressing enough. The spark between the hero and heroine was electric, but they can't seem to have a meaningful conversation. The secondary characters are cardboard, without real emotion. You bump along and hit the potholes, and you're forced to stop and examine the road. Did you go the right way? Should you have turned left at the corner instead? Will you run out of road before the planned trip is over?

This is the serious stuff you need to deal with to make a great book. By the time you near the finish line, you'll fall back into a full love affair. The kids are grown, you're retired, you're rich, and you finally get time to yourself. You see the threads coming together, and you can soar to the end.

Giving up too soon is dangerous. If you chase the shiny, new idea each time, you lack staying power and you won't be able to write a full, meaningful book because you only write the easy parts. How can you create a proper character arc without some degree of growing pains for your characters? And for yourself?

Now, I'm not saying your book sucks if there aren't bumps or bruises. Some books are just gifts. But if you're jumping ship each time you encounter problems, you need to look at your motivation.

New writers: Finish the book you're working on. It's the only way to find out that you can do it again. It's a way to earn your Scout badge and to show you have the perseverance needed in a world that may eventually rip your heart out and do a happy dance all over it.

One of the most beautiful phrases I know besides *once upon a time* is *the end*.

Pick the story that pulses in your gut. Then do everything in your power to finish the book. Even if you realize you made a mistake. Even if you realize it's a sucky book, it won't sell, or you've suddenly lost all interest.

Finish the book. Then make your decision to revise or move on to the next one.

A story unfinished is a sad thing. It screams of potential not realized. It sobs with what could have been. Stories need closure, for readers and the writer. Since you are the only one to see this story, do what needs to be done.

Finish the damn book.

··············Exercise··············

Have you ever quit on a book? A short story? An essay? A poem? Why? Do you regret it, or did your decision to begin a new project prove helpful? Assess your body of work and how often you quit. If you feel like it's damaged your career, make an intention to finish something completely—good or bad. Your Muse needs to know what it's like to type "The End." Stories need closure. So do writers.

··

commit to marriage; avoid the affairs

8

trademarks of best-selling authors

> *"The work never matches the dream of perfection the artist has to start with."*
>
> —WILLIAM FAULKNER

I'm an author stalker.

Can't help it. There's something about coming face-to-face with a favorite author. I feel my breath catch, my heart speed up, and my fingers shake. I'm afraid to approach, but I introduce myself and thank them for their work. My words are polite and dignified. If they only knew I wanted to hug them fiercely with fan devotion, it would scare the crap out of them.

Listening to best-selling authors gives us hope. Many times, we think these writers carry the keys to breaking out. As a proud author stalker, I've followed poor Susan Elizabeth Phillips into the ladies room at JFK International Airport, just to be close to her and her shimmering magic aura of creativity. I've attended almost a dozen of her talks, because I learn something new each time.

Allowing yourself to be open to advice or ideas from other authors is important for growth.

Writing comes in stages. At one point in my career, I listened to a workshop on theme and walked out halfway through. Simply put, it was over my head. I wasn't ready. But a few years later, Suzanne Brockmann delivered a talk on theme that blasted my writing to the next level. It was like a million lightbulbs exploded, and I finally *got it*.

As my career grew, I was lucky enough to be the one behind the table, sharing *my* knowledge and advice. Throughout my travels, I've gained valuable friendships that have been critical to keeping my sanity. I also learned that after talking to numerous best-selling authors, many of them brought the same lessons to the table. It became fascinating to me, and the idea of combining all of these amazing lessons into one streamlined list was exciting. After all, we can't always travel to all the conferences or read individual author blogs daily. I always dreamed of gathering a huge group of authors I loved and respected in a room and picking their brains, authors who had hit the best-seller list and carved out a steady career in an industry filled with uncertainty, authors who had guts and vision, and were savvy and able to write on a full-time basis.

I decided this would be a workshop I wanted to present at conferences. I surveyed over fifty best-selling authors whose books made it onto best-seller lists like *The New York Times*, *USA Today*, or both. These authors go beyond the Top 100 on an Amazon category. They've been able to sell the necessary number of books to hit the list, which is extremely difficult to do. Most of them have achieved this numerous times.

In doing research for the workshop, I asked these authors to rank the major components they believed were critical to not just reach best-seller status, but to maintain it. In addition, they added individual, specific advice and comments they believed were necessary for the journey to success.

The results were turned into a workshop called "The Trademark Secrets of Best-Selling Authors." I've taught this workshop with Laura Kaye at RWA, where we broke the secrets down into the following categories: Writing, Publicity & Marketing, Networking, and Approach to Business.

I've listed the breakdown in this chapter, but I also dive deeper into some of these categories, which I've made into individual chapters in this book. You'll also find tons of quotes that I share from some of the best in the business.

WRITING SECRETS

Readers Love Characters

- If readers fall in love with your characters, they will follow them through an entire series.
- Series and sequels are important in building readership.
- If readers identify with your characters, they are more likely to take a leap with you into other series and other genres.

I had so much to discuss about writing great characters I dedicated an entire chapter where I give my personal viewpoints. Here are some thoughts from a few authors:

Writing Advice

"Building powerful characters is something I hear echoed again and again in reader mail. In fact, I've just begun a mystery series with a character I first introduced in a romance series nearly ten years ago, simply because I kept hearing over and over again that readers wanted to see more of him. This made me want to see more of him, and gave me an idea, which built into an entirely new series. My books are all character driven, and it's the characters that keep readers coming back for more."

—Alyssa Day, *New York Times* Best-Selling Author

"Characters are the vehicles that transport emotions—we feel what they feel. Characters should be relatable but interesting and fantasy fulfilling. Even with stand-alone books, if readers know that you, as an author, are capable of giving them enthralling characters, they'll be eager to read any book you write next."

—Emma Chase, *New York Times* Best-Selling Author

"I caught a trend. I have a unique voice. I found a publishing house that truly saw the potential in my books and put their publicity and marketing powers into supporting me. Those are the things that *launched* my full-time writing career. What *keeps* my books on the best-seller lists boils down to one thing and one thing only: I work very hard to create characters that enthrall my readers. When writing suspense or romantic suspense, most people want to talk plot. And that's important. The plot is what moves the story forward. But you can have the greatest plot in the world, and your book won't sell diddly-squat unless readers become invested in the characters that plot is centered around. Big, bold, complex characters keep readers coming back for more. And more. And more ..."

—Julie Ann Walker, *New York Times* Best-Selling Author

"You're watching trends, ready to jump on the bandwagon of billionaires, military heroes, and bare-chested covers! I highly suggest slowing down, stepping back, and figuring out what you are most passionate about writing. Passion conveys on the page, and your strongest writing will come through in the stories you want to tell, rather than stories that fit a current (ever-changing) trend. If you're writing romance, and you don't fall in love with your characters, how can you expect your readers to?"

—Melissa Foster, *New York Times* Best-Selling Author

Emotion

- Emotion is the key to creating an immersive experience.
- Emotions you want to evoke include arousal, fear, anger, amusement, humor, vulnerability, enthusiasm, anticipation, hope, happiness, and sadness.

This is another important topic that I dedicate a whole chapter to. Enjoy these great quotes:

Writing Advice

"If you deliver an intensely emotional experience for your reader, they won't forget. Personally, the books I love the most pack a wallop—I laugh, I cry, I get angry, I sigh. And I don't forget that author. I'd rather read one highly emotional book a month than ten books that just don't go deep enough. I spend more time trying to examine character emotion than any other aspect of my stories."

—Kristan Higgins, *New York Times* Best-Selling Author

"Infusing emotion helps create the experience for a reader."

—Brenda Novak, *New York Times* Best-Selling Author

Powerful Hooks Keep Readers Reading

- From premise to chapter endings, write every part of your book with a hook in mind.
- Make sure your hook is solid and real; no one likes to feel cheated if the hook doesn't pay off.

This is another topic that I've included as a chapter in this book, but how about an example? Let's take this particular chapter. The title is Trademarks of Best-Selling Authors. The hook is that I'm going to reveal the special secrets that best-selling authors know. Exciting and juicy, right?

When a reader gets to the end of this chapter, she will decide if I kept my word. If I delivered on my hook, the reader will feel satisfied. But what if I gave her a few bullet points, no quotes, and no real explanation?

Well, she'd be pissed off. She'd say, "That Jennifer Probst promised me something, and she didn't deliver." And I bet she wouldn't buy any of my books. So, delivering on a great hook is just as important as offering one. If you promise a reader a story with lots of juicy sex, and you give them closed-door bedroom scenes, readers aren't only going to refuse to buy your other books, they'll make damn sure to tell all their friends.

Writing Advice

"An effective opening hook can make the difference between a reader staying with your book or putting it down. Before I started writing fiction, I worked as a newspaper reporter. My entire first year, the news editor drilled into me the importance of grabbing the reader's interest early and not burying the best information deep in the story.

What makes a good hook? It doesn't need to be a gimmick. The key is to convey tension and conflict, even if it's subtle. It needs to be just enough to snag the reader's attention. By the end of page one—or better yet, paragraph one—you want your reader to sense that something is amiss in the character's world. Plant that seed of curiosity early so the reader will turn the page."

—Laura Griffin, *New York Times* Best-Selling Author

"I think if I wrote more books with a hook in mind, some delicious encapsulated conflict or idea that makes the book impossible not to buy, I'd sell more books. You can hang a lot of things on that—great characters, rich emotions. But a hook that helps marketing sell the book—helps sell lots of books."

—Molly O'Keefe, *New York Times* Best-Selling Author

"For years, I've studied some of the truly impressive best-selling authors and I'm convinced that the secret to an incredible, lasting career is to not just write a great book, but to write a 'sticky' book. Some authors simply know how to keep a reader glued to the page and hungry for more when they've finished. Frequent releases with gasp-inducing hooks and eye-catching covers all backed up with expensive and extensive marketing efforts can and do rise to the top of the charts. But the real trick is to get that reader to come back again and again, and that secret is buried in compelling storytelling, unforgettable characters, and a compulsively readable voice. Some people might even argue that the writing isn't 'quality' or the craft isn't 'perfect,' but the fact is, readers gobble up every word, talk about it to their friends, and wait impatiently for the next book. That's the secret to success!"

—Roxanne St. Claire, *New York Times* Best-Selling Author

Meet Reader Expectations

- Know your target audience.
- Know who you are and what you represent to your readers; understand the responsibility that comes along with that.
- Answer these two important questions:

    1. What is your goal?
    2. Who are the readers who will likely buy your book?

Know thy reader. That's my contribution. But these authors say it much better:

Writing Advice

"One of the things I've learned in building my own series is that consistency is the key. I write genre fiction—specifically romantic suspense. I set out to write a series, but also to build a brand. I never finish a book without beginning the next one. My 'epilogues' are truly a preview of what comes next. They feature the next hero and a glimpse of the adventure to come. Not only does this tell the reader what to expect, it hopefully leaves them wanting the next book in their hands. Be constant in the material you give a reader in the course of a series. I'm not saying write the same story over and over again, but there are a few elements that should remain the same when writing a romance series. There should be a happy ending. There should be roughly the same level of sex in every book. If you're writing erotic and suddenly the next book in your series contains nothing but a kiss, readers notice. The same is true of a sweet novel that suddenly has a ton of exotic play. You will get letters about that and not the nice kind. The last thing I'll say about consistency concerns release schedules. I try to be consistent in when I release a book out into the wild. For the last several years it's been February and August. Readers know that's when they'll get a big book from me. I put out release dates well in advance and I do everything I can to make them. This is my business and I attempt to run it in a consistent manner. One of the things I've learned in the last five years is that hard work trumps talent. When you combine the two, you can have a career to be proud of."

—Lexi Blake, *USA Today* Best-Selling Author

"Readers know what they want. If you listen to them, then they have respect for you, and they are more forgiving when you want to try a new adventure. Remember your fans. They can make or break your career."

—Melody Anne, *New York Times* Best-Selling Author

PUBLICITY AND MARKETING SECRETS

Discoverability Is Your Top Priority

- Know the difference between publicity and marketing.
- No one will read your book if they don't know about your book.
- Constant, consistent marketing effort will generate buzz.

Writing Advice

"Bottom line? No one will buy your book if they don't know about your book. Getting the word out there is important. When I switched genres to erotic romance, I shared six chapters of the book on my blog and Facebook. It got people excited and talking about the book before it was out. The book was my first *New York Times* bestseller. Hopefully readers would have found it anyway, but that early buzz was especially helpful during release week."

—J. Kenner, *New York Times* Best-Selling Author

write naked

"I'd say that getting to the top and staying at the top require different strategies in this day and age. There are so many books, so many authors, that great publicity and marketing skills are a huge plus. To make your mark, you need a constant, consistent marketing effort."

—Rachel Van Dyken, *New York Times* Best-Selling Author

Rachel's right. It's hard enough to get there, but staying at the top is even harder. A mix of marketing is critical. Tracking what works is also important, which is easy to do with technology. Boosting posts, social media ads, and Book Bub ads can give you solid numbers to look at. You'll also want to stay in the spotlight between releases, so readers don't lose touch with you. Engage in social media as a person, not just an author.

There is a key difference between marketing and publicity. Marketing focuses on specific ways you reach readers to sell your books. Publicity is gaining awareness through the media and is a subset of marketing. Using both of these methods in various ways is important in growing your audience.

Looking for ideas? Try reading your first chapter as a video on YouTube or Facebook Live. Create a Goodreads Q&A. Attend a Skype book club session. Sign up for an author takeover at a popular blog. Book unique print or online ads at various outlets.

New York Times best-selling author Ruth Cardello once told me she tries something different once a week. She wrote a letter to Ellen (DeGeneres) one day. She introduced herself to a library on another day. She threw a party for her street team. Her point is to think outside the box. You have little to lose.

Many business strategies work well for authors, but making the first book free in a series still remains a popular strategy. *New York Times* best-selling author Marie Force says, "Other than writing engaging books that connect with readers, the most important thing I did to put myself on the best-seller lists was to offer first-in-series books for free. Nothing I've done has resulted in the kind of residual sales that free books have provided. The 'loss leader' is a well-regarded tactic in business, and it applies to our business as well. Free books introduce you and your work to readers who never would've tried you otherwise. Freebies often result in readers who go on to read your entire catalog and buy every new book the day it is released. I never feel like I'm 'losing' anything by giving away a book for free and then collecting thousands of follow-up paid sales."

If you're going to try this strategy, be sure to have at least three books in a series before making the first book free. Many authors say this is the best way to achieve results.

Networking Is Vital

- Bloggers are key influencers.
- Remember that bloggers are highly in demand, get more requests for reviews and promotion than they can fulfill, and are largely unpaid.
- Social media helps cement relationships and can help build connections with other authors.
- Use assistants versus direct communication with authors and readers.

Let's be honest. When you're asked to write a blog and make book recommendations, you have a few go-to books you always cite. I round out the list with books I purchase by authors I know, or authors who I feel like I have a real relationship with. It makes my connection to the book stronger. I'll recommend them over someone else's book every time.

Boxed sets are a great indication of what good networking can do. Pooling talents of other authors and bundling stories is a brilliant marketing tactic. Networking is one of the most important ways to build and maintain a successful career. Networking doesn't have to be sleazy. It's not, "Here's my card, call me," or boasting about how you've met so-and-so. Networking is about *maintaining* the relationships with the people you meet. Let people get to know you, and they'll recommend your work when opportunities arise.

Make sure that if you use an assistant, you still remain the principle voice of your social media outlets. Readers who are consistently blocked by an assistant may lose connection to the author, and therefore, have less interest in purchasing books. Asking your assistant to reach out to network with another author is not as powerful as making the initial introduction yourself. Be smart about when to use your assistants to increase productivity, and when it's best to take the time to make your own outreach.

Writing Advice

"Readers come first. Then fellow authors. Then people working in the publishing side of the industry. Connecting with fellow authors grows an author's reader base and keeps them up to date on industry changes. Connections with key people in the industry can increase the author's visibility and therefore gain the author a larger audience. But it all starts with the readers."

—Ruth Cardello, *New York Times* Best-Selling Author

"Bloggers are the new gatekeepers of romance. In order to be successful you need to network with the bloggers [and] also participate in blog tours, cover reveals, blitzes, etc. Networking with other authors is just as important. Where one of us succeeds we all succeed. It's about sharing, supporting, and encouraging one another. The business is big enough for everyone."

—Rachel Van Dyken, *New York Times* Best-Selling Author

"Build and nurture relationships. Publishing is a long-term business and writers should focus on the next book, but also on building relationships for long-term. Nurture relationships with your readers. They are precious! Take care of bloggers and reviewers who support your work. Foster healthy friendships with fellow writers. And, absolutely, positively, work to develop strong partnerships with retailers. By that I mean be a good team player! Have something to offer a retail partner, and strive to take time, care, and energy when reaching out to your partners. Those relationships will pay off over the course of your career."

—Lauren Blakely, *New York Times* Best-Selling Author

Readers Want to Know You

- Consider what you can do to stand out to readers, to make a lasting impression.
- Make readers feel as if they're invested in your success.

Writing Advice

"I remind every author I meet that it will take a reader seven to ten times to hear their name before they pick up their book. How many times did you hear their name ... see their name ... talk to them at a conference before you actually cracked the book? Networking starts from the moment you decide to be a writer. Because writing for yourself is kinda like daydreaming. It's nice and all, but if you do it too often, people are gonna think you're crazy! 'Nuff said."

—Catherine Bybee, *New York Times* Best-Selling Author

APPROACH TO BUSINESS SECRETS

Think Career, Not Hobby

- Treat your writing as a product necessary to your career, rather than a gift to share. Make business decisions that help sustain a career, not a hobby.
- Post the words "I am a writer" on your wall. Not "aspiring" or "unpublished," but "a writer," because you write on a regular basis and finish projects.

Writing Advice

"After starting the next book, and the one after that, it's most important to honor your contract. If you say you're going to get a book turned in on a certain day, ensure that happens. Also, know when to pick your battles. Authors have to understand what leverage they have and when. Making too many demands early on, whether justified or not, only gets you negatively labeled."

—Lori Foster, *New York Times* Best-Selling Author

"From the very beginning, I decided I would treat my writing as a full-time job—because that's what I wanted it to be. I wouldn't wait for an elusive muse to inspire me. I would write whether I wanted to do so or not, until I met a daily goal. In doing so, I trained and prepared myself for the deadlines I would one day have."

—Gena Showalter, *New York Times* Best-Selling Author

"In October 2013, I released the seventh, and supposedly final, book in the Songs of Submission [series] (turns out I had two more in me). I had a full-time job as a knit technician. I was making $75,000 a year and was so good at my job I could get in at 10:30 A.M. and leave at 4 P.M. without missing a thing. I loved my boss and my co-workers. If I was going to stay at a job until retirement, this would have been it.

write naked

But every hour I spent talking about sweaters with someone in China, I was losing money, and when that sunk in I hung up my tape measure for good.

Some people don't have the luxury of leaving their job, but for me, once the stakes were raised on this career I stopped futzing around and got real.

For me, that meant sinking money into the business.

When I quit in December 2013, I probably hadn't done more than four giveaways. I didn't have many romance writer friends. I designed my own covers, had a fan do the formatting, and didn't have a website. I designed book covers on the side, because I was terrified. Ecstatic, but terrified.

I can't tell you everything I did, because I barely remember, but as I've gone on, I've become better at seeing this as a business. Yes to giveaways. Yes to marketing. Yes to advertising. About 20 percent of my gross income goes back into the business in the form of marketing and advertising.

I hired people. I fired them. I change daily.

Maybe you can't quit your job right now. That's totally cool. I know very successful authors who keep their jobs for all kinds of reasons. But you can still set aside a portion of your gross income for your books. Whatever it takes. No amount is too small. Spend it. No business can run on one person's energy alone."

—C.D. Reiss, *New York Times* Best-Selling Author

"I've learned a lot of great advice along the way, some from my peers, and others from failure. My most recent aha moment is that it's okay to say no. Setting boundaries early on with everyone—colleagues, friends (new and old), spouses, publishers, editors, agents, and readers is not only okay, it's empowering. Say no to distractions. Say no to any outside influences of your manuscript that don't feel right to you. Say no to others dictating your characters' journey. Say no to any demands for your time. Say no to expectations of perfection—especially from yourself. Say no to allowing others to take advantage of you, your hard-earned money, or the money-making power of your audience and your brand. I was raised in rural Oklahoma, and I've felt until recently that saying no was an insult. Turns out others rather respect you for it. If you cross paths with someone who's upset by the word no, it's likely they didn't have your best interests in mind, anyway."

—Jamie McGuire, *New York Times* Best-Selling Author

Smart Business Goals

- Be professional.
- Think long-term—it's a marathon, not a sprint.
- Join professional organizations; associate with other professionals.
- Produce a great product first. Smart business plans may differ but it comes down to product.

Writing Advice

"Write down your goals and check in with yourself once a month. For me, writing them down is like a commitment to myself, and when I reassess every month, I have to be honest with myself about what I accomplished and what I didn't. And I'll add that if you share this list with a trusted friend, there is even more accountability for you"

—Robin Covington, *USA Today* Best-Selling Author

"Don't wait for your muse. She doesn't write the books. You do."

—Shayla Black, *New York Times* Best-Selling Author

"Most writers write every day. Or at least every weekday, or some set schedule. And since this is a job, I also make it a requirement that I spend some time each week doing nonwriting related stuff, like promo and networking. I have to be careful to not mix that up with just chatting with writers online. I have to do some focused chores, like getting a newsletter done. I'm constantly learning, evaluating, and re-evaluating what works and what doesn't."

—Tracy Brogan, *New York Times* Best-Selling Author

"If authors stop treating their book as a popularity contest, and think of it as their living, they will do things differently. Making the top one hundred on Amazon for a day or two with a ninety-nine cent book does not a writing career make."

—Raine Miller, *New York Times* Best-Selling Author

"Trusting the right people, making decisions based on my own criteria not others. Making decisions based on information instead of emotion. Consistently handling myself as a professional."

—Molly O'Keefe, *New York Times* Best-Selling Author

"I'm a firm believer in the saying 'the imagination is the preview to life's coming attractions.' I knew right from childhood that I wanted to write, but let reality get in the way for years. When I finally started writing, I sucked. Terribly bad. I read the book *Think Rich, Grow Rich* by Napoleon Hill, and a lesson really stuck with me. He said to write an affirmation about what I wanted most in life and what I would do to achieve it. Then I was to repeat that saying over and over again throughout the day. I did. It took a few years before I saw results, but my affirmation was, *I am determined to have wealth through writing. I'm prepared to give my utmost into books that people enjoy and won't stop until I've achieved my dreams.* Even to this day, I still repeat it. It's become second nature and trained my brain to remain positive, focused on my business, and confident that what I can dream can be achieved."

—Pepper Winters, *New York Times* Best-Selling Author

"I think my success was kind of a perfect storm of things. For one, I wrote to entertain myself (and still do) because I figured if the story kept me reading, it would do the same for others. Second, my business model is based on something my father taught me a long time ago: Scared money never wins. You have to be willing to take risks in order to reap rewards. Doing my own audiobooks was a big investment, as was the coloring book, but those things have not only paid off, they've increased my brand. Which leads me to the third element: branding. I am my brand, and my voice is authentically mine. I believe that resonates in the writing. Lastly, I genuinely love my readers. They are the reason I write and I do my best to respond to each one who takes the time to contact me."

—Kristen Painter, *New York Times* Best-Selling Author

Positivity

- Believe in yourself.
- Be a positive force in the social media world.
- Be judicious about what you share.
- Opinions are often a luxury an author cannot afford to have when it comes to politics, world events, or the quality of another author's work.

Writing Advice

"Believe you are going to succeed. Which means having a positive attitude in the face of overwhelming odds which say you should and will fail."

—Bob Mayer, *New York Times* Best-Selling Author

"There are multiple paths to the same place. You have yours. If someone else's seems to be smoother and sunnier and lined with more roses than yours, it's only because from where you're standing you can't see their rough spot and rainy days and steep hills and dark valleys. Just stay on your path, wear good shoes, carry an umbrella, and keep your eyes on where you're going."

—Erin Nicholas, *New York Times* Best-Selling Author

"You can be the ripest, *juiciest peach* in the world, and there's still going to be somebody who hates peaches."

—Dita Von Teese

Take Calculated Risks

- Write the book about which you are passionate.
- Own and develop your unique writing voice.
- Don't chase trends.
- Push the envelope and stretch yourself in your writing.
- Don't live in your writing comfort zone.
- Do the thing that scares you.

Writing Advice

"Protect the Muse, give her time to give birth to your ideas, and nurture them before you seek the opinion of others. Your book is yours. Own that always! And remember no one can ever be better at being you than *you* can."

—Katy Evans, *New York Times* Best-Selling Author

"Be unique: I firmly believe that by embracing what makes us and our writing different from everything else, we create a market for our books that only we can fill. When people ask me what they can do to help ensure their success as an author, I tell them to find what makes their writing unique ... and be bold with it. Give readers something only you can give them, whether that means your distinctive voice, your unique fictional world, or your exceptional ability to evoke emotion. Whatever it is that makes you stand out, use it, own it, and go all out. You want your name to be one people associate with witty dialogue or demon-run hospitals or historical accuracy ... find your 'thing' and corner the market!"

—Larissa Ione, *New York Times* Best-Selling Author

"I think an author has to write what scares them. The more you dare yourself, the less likely it's the same song and dance the readers have encountered before. The hero in one of my novels is a homeless man, and it's by far my most successful one."

—Debra Anastasia, *New York Times* Best-Selling Author

"I have a friend who said, 'Self-delusion is so much more productive than self-doubt.' If I had looked at the odds, I would have given up before I even started. But I dared to take a risk. It's the *only* way to make it."

—Tracy Brogan, *New York Times* Best-Selling Author

"Write stories that excite you, even if they may not be popular, even if there's a chance people won't 'get it.' Like Marilyn Monroe said, 'It's better to be absolutely ridiculous than absolutely boring.'"

—Emma Chase, *New York Times* Best-Selling Author

"Taking risks is rewarded in publishing. Playing it safe rarely is. Write the book you are passionate about. No one else will be passionate about your book unless you're passionate about it first."

—Tiffany Reisz, *New York Times* Best-Selling Author

"I think one of the keys to being a successful, long-term writer is having a distinctive voice—something that makes an author's prose, dialogue, and characters feel fresh and stand out from other books. If readers can open up a random book and recognize the author after reading just a page or two, that's a sign of a distinctive voice."

—Julie James, *New York Times* Best-Selling Author

Examples of career risks vary from moving from a traditional publisher to an indie publisher, or from indie to traditional. Or becoming a hybrid. Or getting an agent. Or signing with a small press. There are endless choices and endless options.

Content risks include changing genres, moving from one length of book to another, putting out more books, creating a serial, writing fan fiction, or writing a book with a cliff-hanger.

I think taking one career risk per year is important to growth—as both a writer and a person.

Write the Next Book

- Writers write.
- Be prolific and publish frequently.
- Backlist is king.
- Be judicious about genre hopping.
- Readers want more, so give them plenty.

Oh, I know. I can hear the groans echoing right now. *That's* the big secret? I hear that all the time. Every day. Blah, blah, blah, we kind of all know that.

It needs to be said over and over for many reasons. Most of the time when I hear things, I'm not ready for them. Or they don't resonate, or the lightbulb isn't ready to click on yet.

More great products mean more great opportunities.

New York Times best-selling author Jennifer Armentrout once said to me there are too many writers who have started series and never finished them. Maybe that's due to lack of interest, low sales, or something else. But beginning a bunch of new series without finishing the ones already out there is disrespectful to the readers you *do* have.

There was one item that didn't show up on the list, but it is my own personal number one secret for becoming a best-selling author.

Never Give Up

- Writers write. That has to be your *main daily activity*, your *driving motivation*, and the words themselves have to be enough. Your love of writing will show through your words.

Writing Advice

"The best advice I ever received was from Mariah Stewart (a *New York Times* best-selling author): 'It doesn't get any easier.' It doesn't matter if your first book hits the *New York Times* list, each book is harder than the last because you want to write a better story for you and your readers. Recognize the challenge. Embrace it. Someone once told me that to 'get published,' you need talent, perseverance, and luck. I think there is some truth to that. To be successful, you need talent (work your craft, create strong characters and interesting stories, and never publish or submit anything subpar), perseverance (don't

write naked

give up, take risks, be bold), and luck (right place, right time for your story). But I believe you make your own luck by always improving your craft (no matter how many bestsellers you've written) and never giving up. Successful writers are successful because they love what they do with a passion so strong they refuse to stop even when faced with obstacles."

—Allison Brennan, *New York Times* Best-Selling Author

"Success is relative. Decide what that means for you, not using the guideposts others do, but whatever you feel would satisfy you and your ambitions. If you can make goals within your control, even better. In other words, you can say: I'll write four books this year because you control your schedule. You can't say: I'll be number one on the *New York Times* because many factors go into an author's inclusion on that list, most outside your control."

—Shayla Black, *New York Times* Bestselling Author

Few people become a bestseller with their first book. When we asked authors which of their books propelled them onto a bestseller list, I received answers that ranged from their first to their forty-ninth.

Another question I never posed? How many rejections did authors deal with before they even got their first book published (*or* decided to self-publish)?

Me?

Too many to count.

If you're *not* writing, submitting, or publishing, you have no opportunity to reach greatness or achieve a personal satisfaction of saying you finished your book.

I go back to these highlights many times when I need to remind myself what is important to being in a long-term career as a writer.

················· *Exercise* ·····················

Go through the list and pick out the top three items you feel are critical to being a writer. Then see how you can make sure you are meeting your goal, in either business or craft. If you see a gap, do one positive thing to close it. Take an online writing class. Subscribe to *Writer's Digest* magazine, or start reading blogs. Take a public relations risk or a career risk. Or start your next book.

···

Special Thanks to All Writers Who Participated in the Survey

- Debra Anastasia
- Bella Andre
- Melody Anne
- Jennifer Armentrout
- Jenna Bennett
- Jennifer Bernard
- Shayla Black
- Jennifer Blake
- Lexi Blake
- Lauren Blakely
- Allison Brennan
- Tracy Brogan
- Kathleen Brooks
- Catherine Bybee
- Ruth Cardello
- Emma Chase
- Alice Clayton
- Kresley Cole
- Robin Covington
- Kyra Davis
- Alyssa Day
- Katy Evans
- Marie Force
- Lori Foster
- Melissa Foster
- Adrienne Giordano
- Laura Griffin
- Lauren Hawkeye
- Kristan Higgins
- Larissa Ione
- Julie James
- Skye Jordan
- Laura Kaye
- Mira Lyn Kelly
- J. Kenner
- Beth Kery
- Christina Lauren
- Sydney Landon
- Lauren Layne
- Jessica Lemmon
- Molly McAdams
- Jamie McGuire
- Jen McLaughlin
- Raine Miller
- Erin Nicholas
- Brenda Novak
- Molly O'Keefe
- Kristen Painter
- Carly Phillips
- Kristen Proby
- C.D. Reiss
- Tiffany Reisz
- Carrie Ann Ryan
- Gena Showalter
- Roxanne St. Claire
- Rachel Van Dyken
- Julie Ann Walker
- Pepper Winters

9

the social media storm

"*Social media is called social media for a reason. It lends itself to sharing rather than horn-tooting.*"

—MARGARET ATWOOD

Let's talk about social media.

A few years ago, some authors were still able to hire companies to do their public relations tasks, but the climate has changed and I think the current model is here to stay. Readers want to hear from authors. Now, if you are Stephen King, James Patterson, John Grisham, Nora Roberts, or J.K. Rowling, you have more flexibility in this capacity. In this case, you can probably become a hermit and people are still going to buy your book.

Ninety-nine percent of the other authors need social media.

This is not a chapter where I dive into the details of the different media available and how to use them effectively. Instead, let's talk about the necessity of social media, what it can do for your career, and how you can learn to live in this world comfortably.

Deep down, I'm a hermit. I suspect the majority of writers are. Being involved in the social world on a regular basis is usually the polar opposite of what writers crave. To do the work—the real work of writing—we need to be alone.

We don't need to carry on a Twitter conversation or worry about the statistics of a Facebook ad boost. We need to sit our ass in a chair in a room with some type of writing instrument and write.

In this new brave world of connection, though, we can't do this *all* the time. Readers are now used to having access to writers, and being able to interact with them about new releases and ask questions about their books. Readers want to feel included in their favorite writers' private worlds. For writers, it's a delicate balance between getting the isolation you need to finish your story while projecting a fun, outgoing personality to the world.

Frankly, I love interacting with readers because it brings me into the light and reminds me of what I need to do. I need to produce great books to make my readers happy. But it's also helpful to allow readers a glimpse into my world.

I remember when I used to read books I loved, hold them to my chest, and wish with all my might there was a way to let the author know she had changed my life. Back then there was only snail mail. Even when e-mail became big, you'd never, ever reach out to an author. It was like picking up the phone to call your editor and ask how her decision on your query was coming along. It was practically illegal.

Now, we writers snap shots of our dogs, children, and bookshelves. We laugh at ourselves in public, post food pics, and funny stories. I believe an author's personality is revealed in each and every post. Think about all the authors you love to follow and what you've come to expect from them.

Some have trademark humor. Some are bawdy. Some regularly post snippets from their daily lives. Some love to post naughty male pictures. Some are sarcastic.

Their writing voice emanates from their posts. This helps reach a reader who may be familiar with their name and may have seen their books around, but never actually bought or read one of their books. A lively post may interest these potential readers to click on their website. I've come up with a list of dos and don'ts on social media, and a way to determine what type of personality you are.

Please know I am not talking about dedicated, targeted Facebook ads or specific advertising. I'm talking about the daily interaction of social media relationships.

Do I believe you will sell buckets of books just for being on social media?

No. Social media is for cultivating relationships, not for peddling your books to anyone and everyone in the hopes of selling. You sell books *organically*. This means being yourself on social media and cultivating a stellar reputation. This stellar reputation only comes to one who is *not* negative, constantly arguing with readers, or engaging in rants. People seek out authors who use humor, radiate positivity, kindness, and share interesting information. Do this and people will come. They will come to peek into your life, be your friend, and laugh at your jokes. If you ever get to meet in person, they will feel like they know you. They will probably buy your books or tell a friend to buy them. But you can never, ever count on sales from social media.

Social media, however, can help you spread the word about your book. You can post about a sale, or about your new release. Or you can talk about upcoming contests or giveaways that you're hosting or that you've heard of. You can post about another author's sale or giveaway or contest.

The key is to sprinkle book-related information around other posts. Cushion the sales pitch.

Now, if you're growing organically, readers will enjoy your business posts, because most likely they have become fans of your work. But if these same readers see your page or feed clogged with *buy me, buy this person*, or *like me*, they will get fed up and stop checking in.

You don't want to be *that* friend. The one who only wants to talk about *me, me, me*, and all their wonderful accomplishments.

The bottom line with social media is to achieve the perfect balance for what works for you as an author. There is no possible way to be on every social media site and still be able to write regularly. Decide what type of writer you are and what works best for your personality. Marie Force orchestrates a wonderful reader survey each year to discover reader's habits and where they frequent online. As of 2016, the majority are still on Facebook, so even if you don't like that social media giant, you need to be on it.

Twitter is one big cocktail party where interesting people pop in to chat, have a drink, and pop back out. Your messages need to be short and sweet, just 140 characters. But Twitter is also my personal favorite hangout. I like short and sweet. Facebook makes me think too much about the perfect post. I feel like I can be sloppier on Twitter and still mange a graceful message.

I link my Facebook and Twitter feed so there's more bang for the buck, and I advise every author to do that.

I'd also suggest creating an account at Instagram, since many readers flock there. Again, I sync to my Facebook and Twitter feed for extra reach. Instagram is based on pictures so it appeals to those who are more visually inclined. Links don't work unless it's a boosted post—which you can do on Facebook—so you need to think on a visual basis and keep it fun and entertaining.

There are many other social sites that you can join.

Tsu is another social media site similar to Facebook, but it seems to have risen slowly and then faded away. At least, for authors who are looking to reach readers.

LinkedIn is a networking site for business professionals, so it's not suited for reaching readers.

Snapchat is fun, but I'm not sure how many readers you can reach using it. Then again, the latest survey shows Snapchat has more users than Twitter, so it may be something to experiment with. Snapchat is based on pictures and is definitely geared toward a younger crowd.

Pinterest is a great way to create boards that highlight your book. Boards are basically blank canvases that you can fill with photos from all over the Internet or in your files. For instance, you can create a board and title it "Hero Inspirations." Then fill it with pictures of Chris Hemsworth, Chris Pratt, Chris Evans, Chris Pine, etc. (Yes, I happen to like men named Chris.) Readers can click on your boards and see what you have posted, and this may lead to interest in your books. I have a folder for each setting my book takes place in, as well as one featuring inspiration for characters, careers, or products.

Google+ is still active.

I'm not sure if Goodreads is considered a social media site, but I advise every writer to be on Goodreads for business reasons. Goodreads is a direct way to reach readers, and you are able to link all your social media, buy links, book trailers, and blog posts to your account.

As this book goes to print, I'm sure even more media hangouts will have emerged, and you may roll your eyes at the ones I listed! The only constant in social media is change.

The key with any media is to do a few things well. I stick with Facebook, Twitter, and Instagram on a regular basis. I use Pinterest only when I'm creating certain boards for my book. I haven't jumped on the Snapchat wagon yet, but I'm testing the waters.

It's important to use social media to reflect your unique personality and voice. If you work with an assistant, make sure they don't post for you regularly. Readers want to hear from you, personally. They feel cheated if they suspect that your assistant posted for you. If they feel cheated enough, they'll stop following you.

I always have my assistant post the promo stuff—teasers, contests, blog tours, and recommendations of other authors. This frees up my time. I suggest making a weekly calendar and spending an hour scheduling posts throughout the week for all promotion and business activities. This will free you up to post social updates whenever you want without worry.

The content and regularity of your social media posts are critical to building a successful foundation. Readers who click on your website and find a blog entry from months ago will be disappointed. In the world we live in, information from last week is ancient, and a reader will most likely leave your page without further study. They need current, interesting, quality posts to keep them engaged.

What type of posts do readers like? How often?

Engage at least once per day. Minimum. It keeps your traffic up, lets everyone know you're alive, and keeps algorithms happy. More is better, but it always depends on the schedule. If I've happened to snap some pictures over the weekend, I upload them to Instagram, link to Facebook and Twitter, and post throughout the week. I don't like to post too much content in one day since I think it overwhelms readers. I go for quality and steady quantity. When I'm writing, I minimize my use of Facebook and Twitter, and check it when I get up to refill my coffee. This sometimes works against me, though, as one thing can lead to another and I may end up avoiding my work. If this happens, I close the apps and don't come back until the work is finished.

Writing needs to come first. At workshops, I always advise writers to watch their social media habits and give themselves a percentage to work toward. For instance, if you feel like you're on social media 60 percent of the time—therefore writing 40 percent—it's time to increase your writing time. Make an honest assessment of where you are, and if your goal is to increase your writing time, then decrease your social media time.

It's great to sell your books and allow followers a peek into your life. But you won't have a career or anything to sell or get readers excited about until the next book is out. One successful book sells another from your backlist. It's a domino effect.

Do you need to mainstream or reduce social media time while you're writing? I find my phone is a great tool for helping me focus when I'm in my office. When I'm out running around, waiting to pick up my boys from school, or in a doctor's office, I immediately log onto Facebook or Twitter, check my feed, respond, and post. Then when I get home, I can dive right into my book.

Another great way of staying active and interesting on social media is sharing funny posts, or ones that depict your personality. For instance, I'm a dog person and I write about rescues, so many of my posts are dog- or animal-rescue related. I like videos of funny pets. I subscribe to BarkPost and The Dodo, and other animal-related sites for up-to-date material. When I was on a journey to lose some weight, I snapped pictures of healthy meals I was cooking, along with recipes. As a mom, I love sharing funny stuff about my kids that won't embarrass them and funny stuff about my husband that *may* embarrass him. Scary Mommy is a great site I use for blog posts about parenting. Inspirational quotes and comical memes build your views, too.

Use other blogs. If I happen to click on a blog post I like, I share it. This gives a shout-out to that author, gives readers another perspective, and keeps your feed live.

If you're trying to determine a good ratio, a nice combination is a few shares, a promo post, and a personal post per day. You can use sites like Hootsuite to schedule easy posts ahead of time, which frees up more of your schedule. Make sure you use common hashtags for Twitter and Instagram to widen your reach. Some popular ones are #amwriting, #amediting, #authorlife, #authorsofinstagram.

Social media isn't a science though. You need to be true to who you are, so if you truly hate being on social media, work smarter. Post every other day, schedule posts ahead of time, or share interesting content.

You can also invite a writer to take over your page for a day, or even an hour. Post what music you are listening to as you work on your book. I use Spotify and create a playlist for each of my books with a particular theme song. Readers love to know what goes on behind the scenes when writers create. My friends also find it interesting. I've been known to post a song of the day.

Get creative, but don't spend so much time trying to create a perfect social persona that your work suffers.

The writing always needs to come first.

If you find you're having trouble prying yourself away from the Internet to write, look for help. There are programs you can use to block websites or certain links for a designated amount of time. One I've found quite helpful is RescueTime, which actually tracks how much time you've spent writing and how much time you've spent ... not writing. Tomato Time is another site that uses a timer for writing sprints with specific breaks built in. I also enjoy doing a #1k1hr sprint on Twitter with some author friends. Send a tweet asking if anyone is interested in participating in a #1K1hr. They might tag you back in a message that tells you they'd like to join. Once you discover a group, pick a time to start, and sprint—that is, write as quickly as you can—for one hour straight, then post your results. I've found this kind of accountability helpful. It's important to know your personality, your writing habits, and your weak spots in order to set up the right tools to help.

The age of social media has brought rock-star status to authors and reams of information to them to help with writing. But the hidden pitfalls in social media must also be addressed.

Instead of being fun, creative, or supportive, it can sometimes drain away a writer's energy. I talk about this briefly in the chapter "Sewage and Blockage." Once, I was struggling with one of my books and extremely frustrated at my inability to write anything good that day. I popped onto Facebook and became overwhelmed by the posts on my newsfeed. It seemed every author I ever knew had finished her book or was experiencing a creative burst and penning brilliance on the page.

I felt the energy literally drain from my body. Depression settled over me. So many authors were cranking out words and here I was, stuck. I sucked. I probably wasn't as good a writer as them, because I'd spent all day writing one sentence, which I promptly deleted. I'm a fraud.

You know the drill. Those pesky voices are always ready to trap you. I walked away from the computer and refused to write for the rest of the day. I felt too crappy.

This happens regularly. It's as if the thing you want the most in the world is the one thing you can't have, and suddenly everyone else has it.

If social media makes you doubt yourself, deflates your ego, dampens your creativity, or generally makes you miserable, *step away from the computer*. You simply need a break. Take a breath, focus on the work, and push everything else out of your mind. There is nothing wrong with removing yourself from the world for an hour, a day, or even longer if the time away helps you protect the work.

Later, when I'm typing, "I reached the end!" in a Facebook post, I know many nameless, faceless authors will curse my existence. It's just part of the cycle. We all hit the ups, and we all hit the downs.

But it's how you handle the downs that is the key to success.

Another pitfall authors question is how personal to get on social media. Again, it depends on the author. Many authors embrace Facebook as a way to truly share, including pictures of their children, family, and the struggles they face. Others feel more comfortable posting strictly about business or lighter topics. I've watched authors blow up their feeds with political and religious posts, and then refuse to apologize for their opinions. I advise you to run your social media sites the way you feel comfortable, but never engage in negative publicity or post cruel comments. Trust me. When you do such things, you risk losing readers. We must think of our pages as our business. Respect and a judgment-free attitude are the best ways to show the world your best self.

I have a personal Facebook page and a business one. I believe authors need to have a separate business profile, even though most of the activity and friends are usually on your personal page. Creating a business page allows you to do promotions and boost posts. You can also reach above the five-thousand friends limit. I know pages that have over fifty thousand likes.

Unfortunately, just because you have a ton of likes doesn't mean people are seeing your posts. Newsfeeds get clogged, and the more pages you like, the greater the chance posts can get lost with the traffic. We can now follow pages, allowing them to be a priority in our newsfeed, but the more active your readers are on your business page, the more exposure you have.

At least once per week I post a giveaway, and many people like and share my post. Again, it's another way to keep my page active. The more interesting or fun your posts are, the more readers want to hang out with you.

The nicer you make your sites, the more people may want to linger. Make sure your banner is updated and eye-catching, detailing your newest release with *buy* or *preorder* buttons and links. Answer all of your messages. Create a tab where readers can purchase your books. Feature your website prominently on the page.

Keep things organized. Make sure your book page shows the series order and offers lots of fun extras, like bonus short stories, book trailers, special reviews, or maps detailing the setting of your book. Keep things professional.

At workshops, I've had beginning writers raise their hands and whine that they're not funny. They tell me they can't be witty in 140 words and they despise Facebook. They want me to admit that writing a great book will be enough, because the readers will come.

The answer? No.

Sure, maybe these writers will get lucky. But if you don't have a social media presence, you're taking a chance that your one shot at intriguing a potential reader will fade into a wisp of smoke because you did nothing to make him or her stay. When I find a new author I love, I always go to their website or Facebook page because I want to feel more connected to them. I want to get the new release news and feel like I'm part of their team. Feeling connected is a human need, one that social media can at least partially fulfill.

If you're interested in working with a publisher, you will be judged on your social media pages. When I sat at auction with New York publishers, every single one of them had already investigated my sites. They were impressed with the setup, my followers, my interaction, and how seriously I took my social presence. They also informed me they had rejected a number of promising authors based on the lack of social media outlets and their refusal to engage. One particular author told one of the publishers her job was not to be on social media, it was only to write.

That author didn't get signed.

My advice is to suck it up and do it. There's plenty of stuff we don't like to do in our jobs. When I was working in an office, everyone hated filing. I hated it, too. But when I was asked to do it, I filed with a smile and a pleasant demeanor. When another department was in trouble, I went to help. The other employees were happy they didn't have to help, but when an opportunity for promotion came up, I was considered because I had stepped up.

You don't have to be a poet, but consider what you like to do in your life and post about that. If you hike, post a picture. If you watch a great television show, tweet using the show's hashtag. Best-selling author Jennifer Weiner live tweets during *The Bachelor* and has become a popular personality—even showing up as a guest on the live after show to discuss the episodes. I've met many new people watching HGTV and the show *House Hunters* through live tweeting, because we have similar interests and love discussing the various homes people buy. This particular interest led to my newest series featuring three heroes that were based on *The Property Brothers*. This combination of work and leisure is important in finding and bonding with new readers with similar interests. Carve out your own niche, and then you won't hate the time spent on social media.

You don't need to sound like anyone else. Bring a unique viewpoint to social media that will engage people. It's like writing. That's the key. Be genuine instead of creating fake posts you think are cool. If you do this, your following will be genuine.

As overwhelming as social media is, it's also a great way to explore new opportunities. Wattpad is a place where you can post your chapters and work for free. Books are now being published this way, by gaining massive support from fans. This is a solid tool you can use to test new work or as a way to offer something for free. You post one chapter at a time and slowly feed it to the community, and they give you feedback.

If you've been playing it safe with social media, it may be time to push your boundaries. When you're feeling uninspired, do one new thing on social media. I'm always surprised at the authors who tell me they ended up loving a platform they'd initially dreaded signing up for.

····························*Exercise*····························

Analyze your social media platform. Is there a major site you're missing and should be on? Or maybe you are on too many of these sites. Do you need to increase your writing time? Create a plan with goals for adjusting the time spent on social media to better fit your schedule. Social media should always be a part of your business plan. Take the time to update your pages' banners to highlight new releases, make scheduled posts, or pick a brand-new site to become involved in. If you are a social media addict, it's time to increase your writing time. Pull back on one or two of those sites and use that time to write.

··

10

networking

"There are secret opportunities hidden inside every failure."

—SOPHIA AMORUSO, *#GIRLBOSS*

Networking isn't only important in this new age of publishing—it's critical.

That's not surprising. Just like the traditional job market, your path can be eased a bit if you know the right people. Sure, you need to have the talent and drive, but solid social contacts can be an advantage.

As authors, our goal is to grow our readership. We try to do this by putting out new releases, standing out on social media, earning great reviews, and making a name to the public. Many writers find it difficult to take their career to the next level. They get stuck at a plateau, in terms of sales and readership, and aren't sure how to continue to grow.

Besides new releases, the second best way to solve this problem is networking.

Cross-pollination of readership is a wonderful way to introduce your books to brand-new readers. You'll want to discover authors whose work is similar to yours and who are also in your genre, and see if they'll give you a shout-out to their readers. (Of course, you'll want to return the favor.) For instance, it's lovely to get a recommendation from a successful paranormal romance author, but since I write contemporary romance, many of her readers won't make the leap over to buy my book.

This is where research comes into play. If you're an established writer, you'll have an easier time making connections with authors you'd like to work with. For beginners with only one or two books, it's a bit tougher. I'd advise going to conferences and stalking … err … following authors you admire to see how they relate to their readers. I also advise perusing the Amazon pages where they list authors similar to you. Bring up your Amazon author page and you will see a section marked: "Customers Also Bought Items By." Then you can research these other authors. You can also bring up your book and see a list of other books readers bought that are similar.

Also, check Goodreads and study other author accounts. Goodreads can link blog posts, book reviews, book trailers, and a variety of other marketing tools to help you learn how a particular author relates to her audience. Join Goodreads groups to meet more readers and authors. Reach out to the authors you discover and tell them you admire their work (if that's true). Genuine compliments always go a long way.

I know I've given out blurbs to new authors because of a beautifully written letter expressing respect and gratitude for my work. Even if I don't offer a blurb, I will definitely remember her, follow her on social media, and be happy to retweet or help promote her book.

Sometimes you still can't reach the bigger authors, and that's fine. Instead, you can try to network with a group of authors who are interested in creating an anthology or a boxed set. Or maybe you'll work with similar authors on a combined giveaway and build your mutual newsletter lists. Or work on a book together. Or even advertise together or coordinate a book signing. Offer to drop into each other's street teams to do a brief takeover. A takeover is when another author visits your group of fans to answer questions, do a giveaway, and entertain your readers. This is a great opportunity to grow your fan base and cement important relationships with other authors.

Opportunities are everywhere, especially if you are polite, nice, and easy to work with. I love working with a variety of other authors on both writing projects and marketing ideas—doing so allows me to find fresh ideas through brainstorming and helps me look at my readership with a new perspective.

One of my newest endeavors combines eleven other authors in an exclusive online readers club on Facebook called "The Dirty Dozen Book Club." A fellow author approached me to see if I was interested in joining a dynamic group that offers free books to readers once a month. It was a brilliant concept. Each of the authors agreed to feature one free monthly read to all members, guaranteeing one year of free reads by twelve different authors. The group has a newsletter list, and sign-up numbers have been high. This is another example of reaching readers in new ways with the power of networking.

But don't use people. Your work with other authors must provide a mutually beneficial relationship. One author may have a bigger readership, but sharing new releases, sales, or giving a shout-out to her book can be your way of holding your own. This is an industry that thrives on give and take. We must remember that there is no such thing as an author too small to work with. Why? Because I've been the author who's grateful for any opportunity. That same author you turn your nose up to today may take off tomorrow, and she'll remember if you were rude or dismissive.

So don't be an ass.

Networking opportunities are not limited to other authors. I always look for new ways to network with businesses. I consistently write one of my most beloved charities, Pets Alive, into my stories about rescue animals. I treasure my work with them, donate shares of my royalties on a regular basis, sponsor their events, and—when I can—volunteer to help walk dogs. This has been a valuable relationship in networking that sprang from my genuine gratitude for all they accomplish.

With a large following on their Facebook page, Pets Alive helps me by posting about my new releases or sharing important information about my books. The organization's members also know me well, and there are always new readers to reach at their charitable events.

Best-selling author Laura Kaye donated two weeks of her proceeds for her book *Hard to Hold On To* to the Wounded Warrior Project. Her novel depicts a hero returning home from war and putting the broken pieces back together. Writing about a passionate subject or charity is a wonderful way to build not only readership, but to bring attention to important charities or businesses.

Think about the issues you are passionate about and get personally involved. Coordinate with organizations to do a speaking engagement. Partner with other authors and brainstorm groundbreaking ideas. The only limits are those you put on yourself.

Asking doesn't hurt anyone. Especially if you ask nicely. I've learned being quiet in business isn't the way to achieve success. You need to go after what you want, and sometimes that means taking a leap.

You will only regret not trying.

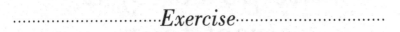

Exercise

Take a moment to go over your social networking circles. Is there a way you can work on a new project with authors you admire? Can you partner with anyone to do a book signing or speaking engagement? Do you want to work with a local charity or organization? Will you attend a writing conference and meet new people who may help you in the future? Can you join an online writing group and become a valuable, active member? Complete a thorough analysis of what you would like to achieve through networking efforts, or what you would like to try for the first time. Then take it step-by-step to make it happen!

11

the power of a street team

'I can't write without a reader. It's precisely like a kiss—you can't do it alone."

—JOHN CHEEVER

I've had many authors ask me about street teams, so I'd like to go over my personal experience with them and take you through the steps of building one.

First off, a street team is a dedicated group of readers who like your work and are interested in helping promote your books. Your relationship with your street team should be mutually beneficial. The readers get to hang out online with the author and receive exclusive material, and the author gets the power of promotion to help share new releases, giveaways, and special events. This is done mostly on Facebook, where access is easier than e-mail lists or Yahoo groups.

When I began to gather readers who would make up my street team, I decided I wanted to grow the group slowly and organically. I didn't want to add a bunch of people in a mad dash to increase my numbers. I wanted the group to be made up of readers who truly loved my work, wanted to help me promote, and were reliable for feedback, brainstorming, or commiseration.

I began with ten readers. I had no specific number in mind for my final goal. My intention to grow the group revolved around recruiting quality members who were excited to be there, and not solely for prizes or giveaways.

I set up a Facebook group page and put my assistant in charge of it. My assistant's main task was to make sure the group ran smoothly. She would also set up giveaways, polls, contests, and help me stay on top of posts. She was not a substitute, though, and when I committed to the street team, I decided to make it a priority to hang out there, regularly post (except for when I'm stuck on a deadline), check in with members on what they are doing or reading, and share new release information, book sales, excerpts of my manuscript, cover reveals, and hold brainstorming sessions regarding my current works-in-progress. I wanted the page to be a fun, dynamic, and always positive place.

I distributed some swag to welcome the original members. I asked them to pick a name they liked for the group, and they chose "The Probst Posse." I put a tab on my website that allows people to request to join the group. Occasionally, I'd give the page a shout-out in my newsletter or on social media, but I never heavily advertised or pushed to grow my member list.

I now have over one thousand members.

Not all of them are active. Some like to pop in when there is an event going on; others are regulars. I embrace them all, and try to keep the page fresh and fun for everyone. While writing *Searching for Mine*, I was stuck on a plot point for my hero, Connor, and I went to my Posse for suggestions. Within an hour, I had over fifty ideas sketched out, and I was able to streamline my story within the next few days. I gave personal shout-outs in the book to the members who provided ideas that I used.

While writing *Searching for Disaster*, I wanted names for two puppies. Immediately, my feed filled with wonderful suggestions. I picked my favorite and thanked this member in the book.

This is a way to get really personal with readers on your own terms.

Sometimes, I also give out advanced reading copies for beta readers and hold exclusive events just for my street team. For my most recent release, *Everywhere and Every Way*, I held my first official book club meeting. Readers asked detailed questions and we discussed the book at length. I also gave away some signed copies.

If you are interested in building a street team or already have one, make sure you engage with and bring new ideas to the group. I found one important item during a reader poll that really helped solidify the purpose of the group.

Members are *not* there for the giveaways.

Yes, the ones who subscribe to your newsletter so they can enter to win a prize—and then quickly drop out—don't have your best interests in mind. But the majority of members are there for the personal interaction with the author. Remember how I talked about interacting with readers? And how as an up-and-coming writer I craved that contact with my favorite writers? Reader interaction is important.

In this case, it helps to think like a parent: Like your children, sometimes readers don't want a cool pen or signed bookmark. They want quality time. That is, they want to talk to the author, ask a question, or find out what you did over the weekend. Give readers quality time and they will be loyal and supportive. When my street team begins promoting a new release, I always see a jump in my rankings within the day.

You can run a street team in whatever manner works for you. You can start small and grow. Just keep the group personal and a safe place to hang out for everyone. This means no bullies, mean people, or trolls. I've only had to block two members in the past several years, and I've never had a problem with negative comments.

I know authors who are very comfortable posting personal pictures on their street team pages. Some don't. There are no rules, except the ones you set up for yourself.

In this new digital world of competition, our readers are treasures. Honoring readers by giving them their own space with you is something they appreciate, and it's a way you can give back.

If you've been thinking about creating a street team, stop thinking and get it done. Start with a few core readers who have posted positive reviews. Create a page, ask them to come up with a cool name, and begin interacting. Let it grow slowly; that way, you won't get stressed out. If you already have a street team, come up with one new idea for the group that your readers will like.

....

12

the indie revolution

"Almost anyone can be an author; the business is to collect money and fame from this state of being."

—A.A. MILNE

Let's talk honesty.

The publishing world is far different from when I started, back when I had wild dreams to be a multipublished, full-time, successful author.

This was before the indie revolution, when there was a strict set of rules that any wannabe writer had to follow. There were multiple gate-keepers who kept an author away from the golden gates. You needed an agent to get a manuscript in front of a solid publisher, but it was difficult to get one if you didn't have experience or a foot in the door. Thus the majority of manuscripts were sifted into the slush pile—your best oppor-tunity to be "discovered."

If you didn't have an agent, you'd submit the manuscript to a publish-ing house, and an editorial assistant would pick through the slush pile in pursuit of hidden treasure.

If that didn't work, you tried to write articles for magazines in order to have some nice credits in your query letter that might tempt someone to pick up the first page of your submission. Or you entered contests where the prize was an editorial or agent reading.

And if that didn't work, well, you kept repeating the same efforts because there were no other options. Usually this included having at least four or five completed manuscripts hidden under the bed since they'd been rejected. You couldn't sell a book with just a proposal if you didn't have a great agent, and even then most publishers wanted to see the entire manuscript before deciding whether or not to buy it.

Today? Opportunities are everywhere. The landscape of writing is full of freedom and possibilities, and there is no ceiling. No real gatekeepers. Writers can now finish their manuscript, fire up the computer, and sell their book the next day.

Pretty amazing, right? Finally, the only real gatekeepers are the reader—we've been able to strip away the middleman. This indie revolution galvanized the industry and baffled and confused publishers, agents, and delighted readers in all capacities. It meant more choices and usually, lower prices.

Let's quickly discuss some important terms used in the industry for clarification purposes. The term indie refers to authors who have no separate publisher involved. There is no middleman except for the distributor. Many use the word indie and self-published interchangeably, since the lines have become a bit more blurred in the past few years.

The term hybrid author refers to an indie author who also chooses to publish in the traditional market—such as Simon & Schuster, Avon, Hatchette, etc.

I consider myself extremely lucky to have experienced both worlds because I appreciate and value the good and bad each of them offers. Knowing both worlds has also helped me adapt and embrace the idea that nothing in publishing stays the same.

This is a great lesson. In life, the only things we can count on are death, taxes, and change. This means you won't get bored, and you'll always have room for growth. The writers and publishers that feared the digital era and refused to change to keep up with readers suffered a loss.

The indie market is the best thing to happen to the industry for a variety of reasons. First, writers have a straight shot to the reader and let her dictate what she likes to read. I had a manuscript rejected because it took place in a vineyard and that setting didn't sell. My editor wanted me to change the setting to a horse-breeding farm and change my hero to a cowboy. No thanks. I let her reject the book because her suggestions changed my story, and it wasn't the story I wanted to write. On another project, I was told dancers made terrible heroines, and no one would buy it.

The growth of self-publishing brought about the explosion in erotica, BDSM, and new adult fiction. In the past, we never would have had a chance to read those stories because the gatekeepers held them back, wagging their fingers at authors and telling them those genres were just not profitable.

Prices became more reasonable for readers: e-books were five dollars or less. The explosion of reading grew to epic proportions, and suddenly people were excited about books again. And you know what genre led the pack?

Romance.

Damn, I'm so proud of this genre. There are so many brave, gutsy women—and men—who took a huge risk and changed the game for the better. I have met lifelong friends who started by self-publishing and became millionaires by busting their asses and learning to be their own CEOs. They mastered marketing, publishing, promotion, and writing all on their own. They made mistakes, started over, and did it again. They never stopped pushing, and the industry is blessed to have such people at its foundation.

Now, let's get back to one of the things I mentioned about the traditional publishing blueprint. Since there were strict gatekeepers, and odds were that your first or even second manuscript wouldn't be accepted, writers were forced to keep writing *new* material and resubmitting.

Personally, I had five full-length books under my bed by the time I was published. I had also written hundreds of essays, and three full-length young adult novels. That's a lot of writing. And it was fair to say, as in any trade, the more you do the better you get. There's a learning curve to writing, like every other career. With each book, my prose grew stronger and leaner, my descriptions fresher, and my dialogue sharper. My voice became stamped with my trademark humor and sexual tension. I learned to write titillating sex scenes. Basically, I developed my craft by writing book after book after book. I had no choice. There were gatekeepers.

Today there is no one to tell you the memoir you lovingly wrote for six months and now published is awful. Readers can be enticed by a ninety-nine-cent steal, open up the book, and be overwhelmed with grammatical errors, misspellings, and bad prose. Like the revolution it was, we overthrew the rulers and, in pure abandoned joy, loudly proclaimed that we didn't need them anymore. "We got this! You can't tell us this sucks anymore—we're bringing it to the people!"

And we did. Oh, we did. I cannot tell you how many bad books I came upon, slapped together with misfit scenes, awful sentence structure, and painful dialogue. That dollar or two I threw away pissed me off. When I used to spend my hard-earned money on a book, I'd be mad if I didn't like it, but I *never* felt cheated. It was rare that a book was poorly edited, lack story quality, and boast a horrible cover all at once. I may not like the writer's voice, or the way the story unfolded, but I never felt the publisher packaged a piece of crap and tried to trick me into buying it. Publishers were strict gatekeepers. They wanted their money back.

But that's how I've felt about many self-published books, especially in the beginning of the indie revolution.

Every industry experiences great highs and shattering lows. The real estate market showered riches on many for years, until the bubble burst and people became bankrupt. The publishing industry has experienced the same rapid growth and decline over the past five years. We have been involved in a revolution, and after the initial celebratory party and surge of riches, balance needs to eventually be restored.

Many writers who claimed success for one book without writing a second have now gone back to their day jobs. People who thought of self-publishing as a get rich quick scheme have now moved on to other endeavors. The market exploded with growth and became glutted. We are now in the process of slowly weeding out the bad from the good, or at least, the career author from the hobbyist.

The flood of self-published works brought wealth to numerous authors, freedom for readers, and diversity in the marketplace. There was a bitter competition between self-published and traditional authors. Many times, it got ugly. The separation between "them" and "us" forced many to claim which side was better, these feuds playing out in online forums and conferences. At signings, separations between self-published authors and traditional outraged both the traditionally published and the self-published. Authors demanded equal treatment, but the industry still reeled at the sudden removal of rules and gatekeepers.

With time, the gap between "us" and "them" has lessened, and I believe the line between self-published and traditional has since blurred. There is acceptance of all formats, and many authors seek the path of true indie writers in an effort to experience the best of both worlds. Traditional publishers used to have a lock on printed titles, but now many self-published authors have brokered deals with distributors and are seeing their once digital-only books in physical form.

But with every revolution, fallout occurs. The market is now glutted. Bookstores, forced to sell other things just to stay afloat, have shrinking shelf space; the future of Barnes & Noble is unknown; and endless digital books are being published on a daily basis. For authors, discoverability has become the main obstacle. The advances traditional publishing houses offer have shrunk. Once healthy, profitable sales for all authors have lessened to a trickle. Many authors who quit their day jobs to write full-time have had to return to those jobs.

Yes, there are still many exceptions. I know a healthy percentage of authors who remain in the game, cultivating large readerships and publishing steadily. These are the career authors who stuck out the ebb and flow of the industry. Not only did they find a way to survive in a changing market, they thrived by consistently delivering quality books and growing their audience. They published multiple series and used the reader-author relationship to push ahead.

Yet, the market is still overcrowded and in desperate need of balance. Readers are overwhelmed with endless free and ninety-nine-cent books, the Kindle Unlimited program, and BookBub deals. Many are snatched up and never read. Many are downloaded, and after a few pages, discarded with disappointment.

To be successful in indie publishing, authors must focus on quality of content.

In short, we need to become our own gatekeepers.

How do we guard the gate with dignity while enjoying the total freedom to write and publish anything we'd like?

Work with a team.

Traditionally published authors are forced to work with a team on their book. I have enjoyed working with Simon & Schuster for a variety of reasons. First, my editor is top rate. Working with her is a growing experience: She's taught me more than anyone else I've encountered in my career. She pushes me and doesn't allow me to become lazy. She's ruthless. Sometimes she's even mean, but when she loves something I know it's perfect. Or at least, as perfect as I can get it.

I have also self-published, working with the partnership of Cool Gus, as I mentioned previously.

One difference I noticed with my self-publishers is the editing. I'm used to being beaten and bloody working with my traditional editor—in a very good way. I'm a perfectionist with revisions, because once that book is in print, I can't change it. With my self-publishers, I can pull the book down, update, add new content, revise the cover if it's not selling, or tweak it in any way. And I can do this at any time. Self-publishing offers a flexibility that I love, but I have to be careful not to get sloppy. It's easy to think the revisions to your first draft are good enough. When I'm slammed with other projects and tasks, I sometimes find my work isn't the best and I need a strong editor to challenge me.

It's important to know what type of writer you are and identify your weak spots. Consistent writing is key. There are many editors you can hire to tear your book apart and put it back together again. I know an author who self-published a book and hired three separate editors to look at it for different issues and places of weakness.

That book hit *The New York Times* best-seller list. She must have done something right.

This is a key advantage to working with a solid team.

Indie authors need to know content editing is different from copyediting. My self-publications are very clean, in terms of prose—the writing goes through several rounds. But in terms of content, I am the boss. And I haven't been able to find an editor that matches my Simon & Schuster editor. If I'm concerned the quality of work isn't up to par with my traditionally published books, I tell Cool Gus I want the book to go one more round of content editing with another editor, just to be sure.

The exception in this story is the amount of years I've been writing. I've put in my hours of practice books. There are still some manuscripts hanging out that I'd love to dust off one day and rewrite, because the concept was fun. But my concern with self-publishing is that with the gates wide open, readers get a stream of so-called writers whose content and product quality is poor. They glut the market with low-priced books, not concerned about whether the books are good quality because it's just a fun hobby and they already have a "real" job. This affects the readers and the publishing business as a whole.

Imagine my frustration when I went to a cocktail party, and someone asked me what I did. I told them I was a writer. The man laughed, nodded his head, and said, "Wonderful, I'm a writer, too. Well, I'm not published yet, but I'm going to write this short book about my life in corporate finance and the sharks out there, and publish it on Amazon. Should take me the weekend. It's fun, right?"

I wanted to die. Or punch him in the face. *Fun?* You think writing is *fun*, you idiot?

"You are not a writer!" I wanted to scream. "You didn't even write the book yet!"

What enraged me most about the conversation was not his bragging about writing a book—I was terrified he'd publish it. I had a feeling it wouldn't go through editing, and maybe readers would actually buy it, and once again, I'd stumble on another article in *The New York Times* about self-published writers' ineptitude at writing decent books, and the poor readers who succumb to the ninety-nine-cent scam.

We need to be our own gatekeepers. I'm not talking about this idiot finance guy. I'm talking about people who bought *this* book and are looking at writing for the long-term—to write, not make a million dollars or get on a reality television show. We need to hold ourselves accountable for learning the craft.

Why is this important? First off, if you publish one bad book, you may not get another chance. If you have the raw talent, you might be forgiven enough that a reader tries your second one. But do you really want to give them another sloppy book and hope they give you a shot at a third?

I've had a few beginning authors contact me regarding their first book. Sometimes I've taken the time to look at new work from an author in an effort to give back to the industry. I know how appreciative I was when I was desperate for feedback from experienced authors. Many of the books I read were not ready for publication. The writing was weak. There was too much telling and no showing. There was sloppy POV and the characters were flat.

write naked

My critiques were gentle, as I pointed out a few specific items they could work on, but I always referred them to a combination of craft books, RWA or writer organizations, or small critique groups. I made sure to give plenty of suggestions, because the quality of writing was the main problem.

Most of them went on to self-publish the book anyway.

Because they could.

Because there are no gatekeepers.

It's frustrating for me to watch my beloved career become belittled. Just because you write a book doesn't mean you need to publish a book. The best thing for a new writer to do is complete at least two books in a row, then go back to the original one and see what can be improved.

If you've grown at all, you'll realize what a mistake it would have been to publish the first book.

Once you decide to self-publish, you must look at it as a business if you want to succeed. Businesses require an investment of funds in order for you to obtain necessary supplies or services to ready your product. Your book is your product. You must take into consideration all the elements that make up your product: cover, blurbs, content editing, copyediting, formatting, uploading, marketing, and public relations—to name a few. Just because you decide to self-publish your book, does not mean you can overlook any of these elements.

Invest in your book. Hire a cover designer. Learn the marketplace so you can make smart decisions on where to publish your book. Make sure your blurb and title showcase your book and offer a hook.

If you are a new writer, I highly recommend hiring content and copy editors to make sure the work shines. In addition, you will need a strong foundation of social networking in place. Research your marketing budget and make smart choices.

You must be a gatekeeper, and hiring a smart team to help is the key.

Cultivate a reputation for quality. It's so much more important than quantity, no matter what you've read about the necessity of publishing three to four books a year to get your writing out there. One amazing, mind-blowing book per year is okay if that's what you're capable of. Look at Susan Elizabeth Phillips. She's honest and admits she cannot write fast. It's not who she is. I don't care if the woman requires three years between books, I will buy them when they release. It may be much harder in this new digital climate to break out with just one book per year, but it's not impossible.

Now, an author who's just starting out may publish just the first book, but have the second and third already written. This way, she guarantees higher quality since she's completed additional books, plus her publishing schedule can be aggressive.

Life has no guarantees, and neither does writing. Just because your previous three books made *The New York Times* best-seller list, there are no guarantees you'll hit it again. Ever.

There is no security in writing. Contracts offer security only for a limited amount of time and a specified number of books. There are no advances in the indie market. When you publish your book, you figure out how much you're going to make that month. To reverse your gloom, you should remember that you might make more in a month than you ever would on a 25 percent royalty rate.

There is another nugget of gold within indie publishing that every author adores: the power of the backlist. Backlist is everything. Traditional publishers mainly focus on new releases. They gear up with marketing and PR plans, schedule phone conferences, ask the author to flood social media and develop ads and create blog tours that cram your newsfeed, etc. Then, one month later, it's all gone. Your publisher seems to lose interest, as if the most powerful sales have passed on and they need to focus their efforts elsewhere.

Unfortunately, that's business. I think it's bad business, but with the number of new releases they juggle each month, they don't have the manpower necessary to consistently sell your backlist.

But *you* can.

Especially with indie publishing. No book is ever dead. My first novel, *Heart of Steel*, which I retitled *Executive Seduction*, has had nine lives. It was published, died, republished, died, and self-published to a healthy cycle of growth and sales depending on how I focus my attention on it. A BookBub ad skyrocketed that sucker to the top 100 in iBooks and Amazon. Twice. And I'm not the only author who focuses on promoting my backlist. I see many popular authors such as Bella Andre, Melissa Foster, Ruth Cardello, Melody

Anne, and Kathleen Brooks all continuously using the sales for their backlist books to grab readers' attention to their ongoing series.

Indie authors should take advantage of the opportunity to discount their books; creating special sales and discounts on books are the key to selling the backlist. They'll also help sell new releases in a series.

There are many services available that advertise free and discounted books to readers. Authors discount their books and pay a fee to sites, and in return, authors get access to numerous readers via an e-mail where readers can buy the books. Some important sites include BookBub, Book Gorilla, Digital Book Today, The Fussy Librarian, ENT (E-Reader News Today), and The Choosy Bookworm. Costs vary depending on the promotion. You should gather a working list of the best places that offer this type of service and consistently try new ones. At the time of this writing, BookBub is the king. I've seen many authors hit best-seller lists and skyrocket a backlist title onto the charts using BookBub. But it's competitive because there are limited booking slots. Authors have to fill out a form and BookBub will let them know if they have been approved, and the date they have been assigned for the sale. I've known authors who have applied for a slot numerous times without approval, so I'd advise to keep trying if you are initially rejected. Many new services have launched, though, and the landscape is ripe for competition. As a businessperson, you need to stay on top of the marketplace and stay abreast of developments in terms of discounting your backlist.

Another popular way to spike backlist sales is to offer new material in a series that will spur readers to buy the first book. For example, offer a new story *and* discount the first book in the series. Or make the first book free. Win-win. Readers get the opportunity to read two stories, and you have a chance to grab more readers.

If you don't have the time in your schedule to release a new book, try to offer something unique to readers. For instance, I write short stories featuring all my characters from my series and release them around Valentine's Day. I then batch them up periodically and put them in my newsletter for readers to enjoy. Or I write a novella with secondary characters from my series. These strategies keep readers happy, offer new material, and give me an opportunity to sell my backlist.

The magic formula is simple.

There *is* no magic formula.

There is only a lot of hard work writing great stories, trying new things, using social media to get in front of the readers, surrounding yourself with a solid team, networking, being open to new opportunities, and doing your best to stay sane and happy.

Mostly I'm happy because I get to write, but I'm definitely not sane anymore!

Who cares? Sane people are boring; they don't have the courage to run naked into the street, screaming for everyone to stop what they are doing and *read* something they have *just* written because it may just be the most important thing in the world.

Writers do.

Writers get to leave this world in a streak of glory. Whether we hit a list or not, whether we write ten books or one, whether we are successful or not (according to society or our own standards), at least we had the guts to try to figure things out.

Let's just do our best to offer our best. In our pursuit of perfect branding, social media wit, and heft advertising, let's not forget the one element that is key to all success.

Craft.

································*Exercise*································

Go read a craft book. One on your keeper shelf, or a brand-spanking-new one that teaches you something you need to work on or remember. Commit to this career and to learning craft all the time. Simply put, craft is essential if you want to be a long-term, successful author.

··

13

your big pay day

"*Often people attempt to live their lives backwards: they try to have more things, or more money, in order to do more of what they want so that they will be happier. The way it actually works is the reverse. You must first be who you really are, then, do what you need to do, in order to have what you want.*"

—MARGARET YOUNG, FROM
JULIA CAMERON'S *THE ARTIST'S WAY*

Let's talk about money.

I remember my husband and I used to play a wonderful game. We'd pretend we'd either won the lottery or the game show *Survivor*. I preferred the lottery, since we had to do nothing else but buy a ticket and sit on the couch, watching our lucky numbers come up. I also knew I'd never win *Survivor*. I'd be voted off at the first tribal council.

We were kind of poor but able to pay the mortgage, current bills, and food bills. We didn't have savings. A thousand dollars might as well have been a million back then, and tax time was the best time of year, because we always got a refund.

Later the refund would go to paying off credit card debt, which just sucked.

When *The Marriage Bargain* took off, I made money. A lot of money. And when the book sold to Simon & Schuster at auction, I made over a million dollars—just like in my dreams.

This deal propelled me into an entirely new universe. My boys had been using furniture donated by my dear friends. Back then, one dresser fell apart when you tried to open a drawer, but we couldn't afford to replace it. Our house was tiny and slowly deteriorating around us.

I'm not telling you this for pity. There are tons of people who were way worse off, and I always appreciated whatever I had. I'm trying to make a point that I went from living extremely sparingly to having a million dollars in my pocket all because of my book.

We celebrated. We sold our house. We built a brand-new one like we'd always dreamed about. We bought a new car. And we gave away money to people in our family who needed it, which felt just as good as spending it on ourselves.

Let's do the math, shall we? First, the tax man takes 40 percent. Then your agent takes 15 percent, which he or she truly deserves for brokering a great deal. That leaves you with $450,000, which is still an insane amount of money. Now, don't forget that because of your success, you have had to hire an accountant, a lawyer, and either an assistant to help with the massive amount of work you just got hit with, or a marketing firm. You'll want to deduct those fees from now and the future.

You've made history. You won the lottery. And as that book is earning publicity and praise, you're wrapped up in it so tightly, it's pretty damn hard to write. Suddenly, you're not a midlister, quietly working on your next project, or an unknown who can huddle in her cave and play in total anonymity.

Now, you must produce a second book. A follow-up. If that first book was part of a series, it's even scarier. The second has to be great, or at least hold up to the first one. And now you have a team of people on your side to—*theoretically*—help you write, taking care of other stuff you once never had to worry about.

But now the writing has changed. Because you're writing for a big audience. You're writing for your new editor, who spent a cool million or more on your stuff, and you can't let her—or anyone else—down. You now need to fund your new house and still pick up the dinner bills when you're out, because success is attached to your name.

Once again, this isn't a whine fest. I'm not going to lie. It's awesome to have your book skyrocket to the top. Even with all the stress, I loved every single moment the ride lasted. I soaked it in to the highest extreme, because I'm a person who knows lightning doesn't strike twice. Anything could change, so I intended to enjoy myself, and I did.

But after you come down off that high, you're back in your office. And honestly, it doesn't matter if you were facing a wall and now you're looking at a beautiful acre of green, rolling grass. Your muse doesn't care. You're still alone in a room trying to write your book. The difference is that now the voices in your head aren't just those of your characters—they're the voices of everyone who counts on you to continue your success.

Maybe the next book or two will be just as huge. Maybe it'll be only moderately successful. Maybe not.

You'll need to learn new skills after hitting it big, like letting go of expectations. That includes focusing on sales. You can't assume you will always make a killing in sales just because people now know you. When the beginning of my Searching For series published, I honestly believed the books were some of my best work. But readers were still stuck on my first series and didn't seem to realize that this new series was a spin-off. My sales sputtered with the new series.

I lost many sleepless nights worrying about everyone's expectations and how I was failing them. I had to maintain the new house now, dazzle my publisher, and sell books, while also taking on more projects than ever before.

I learned nothing lasts forever, but I wouldn't want it to. I like exploring new series and bringing freshness to readers. I had to realize that making the *USA Today* best-seller list and not *The New York Times* is *not* a failure.

Success means different things to different people. It also changes like a moving target, depending on your current situation. For me, success once meant quitting my day job to write full-time. Then it became hitting a best-seller list. As time passed, success began to morph into a combination of stellar sales, name recognition, steady releases, and big money.

It was exhausting.

And I was the source of my own exhaustion.

The funny thing about being successful is how the ground beneath you doesn't feel as solid anymore. This makes absolutely no sense, since technically I achieved financial security and discoverability—two huge elements of every hardworking author's dream. Yet, I still couldn't control any of my books' successes. I couldn't make them hit a best-seller list, and I couldn't stop any of them from making the top of the chart one day and sliding into total obscurity the next.

That's just something you have to learn to be okay with. The good and bad, up and down, success and failures. If you want to be a career author, you will still feel vulnerable, afraid, and sick to your stomach *even with success.*

Even with a million dollars.

I learned one valuable lesson that helps me get through it all. I focus on the work. I focus on my writing, day in and day out, and when I struggle, I dig deep and write even more. That's how I put the voices to rest. I know I'm not a one-hit wonder or a fraud. I know I'd still be writing if I hadn't made that money, because it's a calling and a gift.

I also learned to be professional. I changed from the kind person who said yes to everyone, signed contracts without fighting for better clauses, and agreed to write too many books in too short of a time into the type of person who thinks like a businesswoman and makes hard decisions. This means saying no. This means sometimes hurting feelings. I always remain kind, but now I ask questions. I decline offers. I'm careful and much more protective of my time, because as many wonderful people as there are, there are still people out there who, like vampires, will drain your creative well dry.

My hope for everyone reading this book?

That you make a million dollars.

Just know there are both positives and negatives that come with everything in this life. You will need to be willing to look at the world—

and your career—in a different way. Understand that you might not be on top forever, unless you are Patterson, Roberts, King, or one of the other top sellers. I'm not saying you can't hit every time. I'm saying the odds are against it, but it's the flexible, hardworking professional who will be in this for the long-term.

Think of the tortoise and the hare. Man, it's fun to win the medal and have everyone celebrate you. But when the cheers disappear, and it's you alone with your book, you need to have the foundation and stamina of the tortoise.

Then you'll earn more than a million dollars.

You'll earn some damn peace and happiness.

······························ *Exercise* ·······························

Your book has gone to auction and you just made a million dollars. Imagine it. Create the moment in your mind. Think about what book it would be, and have fun with the daydream. Now, write in your journal everything you would do with this money. What would you write next? Do you have career goals that reach beyond your book hitting big? You should. Goals keep you firmly grounded to the present instead of daydreaming of the future. If you do the work, you may get this opportunity. Better to be prepared for it rather than shocked and scrambling to build a platform, write another book, or do the thousands of things that are required when you've achieved success. Do it now and be prepared for greatness.

PART TWO

the

craft

of

writing

14

writing is a muscle

"Exercise the writing muscle every day, even if it is only a letter, notes, a title list, a character sketch, a journal entry. Writers are like dancers, like athletes. Without that exercise, the muscles seize up."

—JANE YOLEN

I've talked over and over about doing the work, because it is crucial to being a successful writer.

But our work is different from other people's work. We work from home or take our laptop to small cafés while we drink gallons of coffee and try to create imaginary worlds strangers want to live in. We need to consistently discipline ourselves to begin writing each and every time we sit down. It's exhausting to have to make a clear intention to write *every single day*.

I never feel like I've figured out the secrets to this career. Each time I start a book, I grope in the dark, ignoring the voices that say I can't do it anymore, fighting through the gleeful devilish minions that jump in my head and say, "Let's skip writing today! Let's just watch television and nap and tell people we wrote!"

It's hard to start writing, every time. No wonder most of us give up and return to our day jobs. In our mind, the artist's life is full of fun and creativity, of unknown journeys and adventure. Sometimes it is these things, but at the very core of what a writer is lies something writers don't really talk about.

Boredom.

There's a lot of boredom and minutia in writing. Oh, when the flow is there, it's like a carnival ride of pleasures. But 90 percent of this job is just staring at a screen, forcing words together while praying the dam will eventually break and give us a river. A river of words that make sense and build a story. A story people will actually want to read.

We stare out of windows, fiddle with social media, and refill our coffee mugs too many times. I get excited when I have to use the bathroom, savoring the steps to freedom from my office.

Yet I savor those very same steps back into my safe haven, where I hope the words will come. How odd.

It is a co-dependent, vicious, love-hate relationship. A therapist would probably tell me to break up with my writing muse.

Writers are their own bosses. Sure, an editor may hold them to a deadline, but we hold the ability to meet the deadline. I remember at my day job, there were times when I felt completely confident I'd reached the top of the learning curve. I mastered every task and knew my boss so well I could anticipate how to meet her needs. I ran the department with competence and though the occasional hiccup arose, I mostly felt like I could coast. Sure, I got bored, but it was easy. It was routine. It was the only thing I knew.

I was also held accountable for each and every action. In writing, the only accountability is words on the page. There is no one to beg for sick days, cajole for vacation, or manipulate to get out early during a snowstorm. Sounds glorious, and often it is. Other times, however, I would give anything for someone to tell me to get my ass in gear. A personal trainer brutal enough to bark out: "Ten pages, Probst, or you have to deal with me!" Instead, there's only my dog, who naps in my office and doesn't care whether I write or not.

Writing is exciting because it's new and scary each time. It's a career that keeps the adrenalin running and life interesting. But in order to reach a level of professionalism, we must learn to produce regularly. This could mean four books a year or one. The key to being a career author is consistency, and the only way to achieve consistency is by treating writing like a muscle.

Think about the gym. God, I hate the gym. I have a love-hate relationship with exercise (mostly hate), but I can never argue with the benefits and how damn good I feel when I finally do it. First off, I get a high from the knowledge I did something difficult. I could float through the rest of the day just from the satisfaction of knowing how I spent that precious hour and the fact I didn't wimp out. My body might be sore and rusty, but if I keep at it, my muscles will get limber. Stronger. More apt to take the abuses life throws at me, because they've been conditioned to flex or tighten, depending on the situation. If I exercise regularly, I stop trying to make excuses, because it's now become a habit. I don't have to fight myself as hard each time I put on my workout gear and begin the familiar journey to the gym.

My mind now whispers, "Oh, that's right. We're exercising now. That's what we do."

You need to get into the same frame of mind with writing.

It needs to be done every day—or at least the days you specifically set aside to do your work.

Writing is an art. But it is also a job.

The longer you stay away from the work, the harder it is to begin again. It's a battle warring inside our own minds, from the moment we think about sitting down to write. As Steven Pressfield says in *The War of Art*, it is "resistance rearing up with the sole purpose of distracting you from your goal."

How do you fight resistance and transform the act of writing into something that becomes a part of your daily life? Treat it like a muscle. Work it hard. Rest when needed. Stretch to stay flexible. Repeat.

It's a beautiful cycle of creativity, yet our minds fight us every single day. Physical exercise keeps our bodies healthy and strong. Writing keeps our souls balanced and fulfilled.

Each day, I put my kids on the bus, take care of the dogs, click on *Good Morning America*, and make my coffee. As it brews, I go through my day, preparing myself to meet the upcoming challenges. This always includes writing, though if I'm knee-deep in edits at the time, I keep my focus on revisions. I walk into my office, place my cup on my coffee warmer, and open e-mail. As I click through to see what I missed from the night before, and quickly check Facebook and Twitter, I try to keep in mind that this is just my warm-up. These are my stretches for the day. This is my routine; I cannot question myself. I ignore the internal pleas to do laundry and the phone call from an old friend who begs for a lunch date. I turn a blind eye to my too-long hair that desperately needs a trim, and the lack of Cheerios in the cupboard. These things can come later; life is waiting for me in all its messy, chaotic forms, but right now, right here, my only job is to write.

By 9 a.m., I realize I've reached my social media limit, and I open my new pages. I reread the last few paragraphs, tinker, and get my mind back into my characters. I sip my coffee. I slip on my Bose headphones and turn on my iPod. I always have a specific playlist for every book to help immerse myself in the story. It is eclectic, filled with old classics like Sinatra and Bennett, but also includes my favorites, such as Rob Thomas, Maroon 5, Lifehouse, Imagine Dragons, and Daughtry, and then goes all the way to soul-pumping top hits by Pitbull, Flo Rida, Chainsmokers, and yes, even Justin Bieber. Then, I write.

This is my heavy workout. If I've done it right, I take only brief moments to stretch or refill my coffee. The longer I stay away from the work, the easier it is for life to intrude and remind me of all the other things that need my attention. I face this battle every day, so it's familiar. The majority of the time I win. Other times, I eat my lunch in front of Bravo television and *The Real Housewives* and get lost in the web of the Internet.

An hour later, maybe two, I force myself to walk back into the office. A fresh cup of coffee is within reach. My headphones lay in a tangle of wires, calling for me. I fidget, look at the window, mentally fight with myself. I don't want to write anymore. I've done enough.

But I know I haven't. Cursing, sometimes cranky, I open the pages again, this time slamming my headphones around my ears and glaring at my dog for having to do this again and again. Why is there no end to this? Why can't I just take a nap or snuggle under a blanket and watch Netflix? Don't I deserve some time? Don't I need to concentrate on my family, the grocery shopping, and my hair, which is now hanging in my face and annoying me? Do I really have to do this again?

I read my last paragraph. It's not as bad as I thought. I flip through a few of the last pages, surprised at the banter between hero and heroine. It's witty. Maybe if I just add a touch right here ... and, *boom*, I'm writing again.

I am not always joyful. Sometimes when I go to the gym, I hate the people behind the counter who give me fake, cheerful smiles and the others who crowd in with their toned bodies and bright pink Lycra shorts. I hate their bouncy ponytails and the gleam of sweat on their brow. I climb the stairs toward the treadmill or a yoga class, cursing under my breath, wondering if I should just quit and go home because I haven't lost any weight and it's useless. I find my spot. Put down my water. The teacher greets us, the music starts. I look around and there is energy in the room. I begin again.

You will never get there. *Ever*. You may battle yourself every day, once a week, or ten times per day. But by treating writing like a muscle—one that needs a regular, maintained workout—you stop thinking about it so much. It's something you just need to do.

And you do need to write. When you stop writing, there's a ragged hole somewhere inside your gut, one that won't go away. I wander around lost when I'm not writing. I'm on edge. Or depressed. I don't have a purpose. My mind drowns out any clear thoughts with endless chatter. I get worse with each day. The guilt slithers and poisons worse than a snake. I don't sleep or I sleep too much. I'm not complete.

It's so much harder *not* to write. When I finally give in, my soul takes a long, deep breath and I'm whole again.

There are many reasons to concentrate on healthy writing habits. When you push yourself into a strict writing routine, or practice snatching pockets of time to work, you also build a strong foundation so that the muscle cannot easily tear. Writers are always dealing with rejection, whether they are published or unpublished. The more limber your writing muscles are, the quicker you will get back to work after the sting of rejection. And that sting comes not only from rejections you receive from publishers and agents. It comes from the editor who dismisses your new idea for a series, the blogger too overwhelmed to review your book, or the snooty look of a reader passing your signing table when she finds out you write romance. It never ends, but when you have the work to rely on, the sting glances off rather than penetrates.

There was a difficult time in my life before *The Marriage Bargain* was published. I was working my full-time job, and I'd been submitting a bunch of articles and essays to various magazines. I was excited about the possibilities, because I'd been working hard and really thought I had a shot at getting published.

I came home from work one day after being stuck in traffic for three hours. My boys were little and one was crying. My husband didn't have dinner ready. I was miserable, sick with a cold. There were two envelopes on the table from magazine publishers.

I remember feeling certain one of them was an acceptance letter. I had been steadily writing and submitting for months, pushing past my doubts and trying to believe I'd finally get a break. The knowledge danced in my veins, and my fingers shook as I tore open the envelope.

And revealed two standard rejection letters.

I was heartbroken. I was tired—more tired than I'd been in a long, long time. I foggily remember telling my husband I was very sick and going to bed. I thought about giving up. I had made no money from writing, I spent endless hours I didn't have working for something I didn't know if I'd ever achieve. It was a low time in my life, and I truly believe if I hadn't been working on that writing muscle, I may have stopped.

But it had become routine. My writing muscle was strong. I remember two days later, I trudged into my office, with my battered Walmart desk, cold air leaking through the windows, and a pile of kids clothes on the floor. I sat down in front of my computer that was on its last leg. I opened my manuscript, and grudgingly, just by damn habit, I began to write again.

Nothing but writing can help you during the bad times. Don't look for external validation, like hitting a best-seller lists, kudos from other authors, raving reviews from readers, or publishers who finally want to buy your work to keep you moving forward. Yes, these are all exciting, and yes, they do give hope, but these validations only exist for a fleeting moment of glory and disappear in a wisp of smoke, leaving you completely alone, once again. Alone with the work.

The real value is in the simple act of writing and creating stories that will last. Stories that mean something to you. Work that muscle hard, and it will support you every time.

Writers need to remember not only to strengthen the writing muscle, but also the body. Sitting for long hours is productive for output, but the physical needs of the human body beg for a stretch, fresh air, and a decent meal. The healthier we are, the more apt we are to write better. As Robin Covington urges, "Maintain your health: This is something that I have let go and have seen the negative results of when I don't take care of myself. When you feel better physically, your brain works better and you can be more productive. Now, I'm not a champion bodybuilder and I don't run marathons but I do make it a priority to work out every day and to remind myself to get up and move while I am writing. Then, when I have to [pull] the occasional all-nighter, I can recover faster. I find that I can write longer and my creativity flows when I feel good."

························*Exercise*························

Do ten push ups and five sit-ups. Kidding! Kind of ... Remind yourself to walk or stretch in between long bouts of writing. And drink water. A healthier, stronger body will help you sit in the chair without developing wellness issues. Invest in an ergonomically designed keyboard and mouse to ward off carpal tunnel syndrome. Wear support gloves. Buy yourself some special pens that make you happy. Download new music on your iPod or smartphone. Buy your favorite color water bottle with the words *writer* on it to put on your desk. Invest in your writing muscles the way you'd invest in buying the perfect workout gear.

15

inspirations

"Writing takes a combination of sophistication and innocence; it takes conscience, our belief that something is beautiful because it's right. To be great, art has to point somewhere."

—ANNE LAMOTT, *BIRD BY BIRD*

Writing helps you find the lost pieces of yourself—those pieces that were misplaced, forgotten, or squashed long, long ago. Through words, we may carve a new path for ourselves or recapture the power to own who we are.

Writing brings intention. It is a permanent place to settle and explore who we are in this one tiny moment of eternity.

To create on a daily basis and dedicate endless, precious time to making up stories, writers must have faith in themselves and the stories they are driven to tell. This career allows me to believe in magic and God, because though the work must be done—and it's sometimes a brutal path—I have found my words often take me to a new level of expression and understanding. I can step back after the grueling process, read, and be struck by the wonder of such a gift.

Of course, this lasts only a short while. Then I'm back to picking it apart and judging. Still, a tiny piece of grace and brilliance balances those long periods of confusion and hopelessness.

But the real food for my soul is inspiration.

Where do you get your ideas?

Would you believe that's the number one question writers are asked?

This question fascinates people. To take the kernel of an idea and allow it to grow and sprout within the pages of a book is a miracle. Without the seed of an idea, there is no book. Our all mighty, beloved, bitchy muse, is the one who sifts through all our potential inspirations to eventually cling fiercely to one idea and whisper, "This one is it. I must write this."

My entire life has become an inspiration. If a creative artist is feeling flat and lifeless, inspiration is the food for the soul that will nourish and hydrate. If we lose our bit of magic, we may become wooden. A pale, robotic image of our best selves. We will scratch the surface and never unlock the rusty old cellar that contains our dreams and visions, and eventually, our greatness.

That's creative death.

Writers must pay attention. You need to open up as life unfolds around you. This will keep you full of stories.

Here are some of the places I continuously find inspiration.

READING

Reading in various genres will sometimes act as a springboard to the excitement you need to power your own work. *I want to be that good,* I think to myself as I read a brilliant passage from another author. *I need to work harder to create such magnificence.*

I love this quote from Kyra Davis, a *New York Times* best-selling author:

To be a truly successful writer you need to be a voracious and eclectic reader. If you're writing romance and all you're reading is romance, there's a good chance you're going to end up writing a romance that's very similar in format, style, and tone to all the other romance novels out there. In a market this crowded, you can't afford that. So pick up a Donna Tartt, an Anne Rice, a David Sedaris, an Elizabeth George, and any other book written by a respected author outside your genre and figure out what makes their books sing. Use that information as both inspiration, or even as a loose guide, for creating something very original within your specific area of fiction.

MOVIES AND TELEVISION

Movies and television have inspired some of my most passionate ideas. I decided to create the Billionaire Builders series because of my obsession with HGTV. Whether it's *House Hunters, Property Brothers,* or *Fixer Upper,* I'm fascinated with the process of building and making things new. So I created the Pierce brothers and their family business, which has been passed on from one generation to the next, and they allow me to live in an HGTV world.

Television series have reached an all new level. When I watch *Game of Thrones* or *The Walking Dead,* I'm able to break down how an episode is created with a specific character arc. It has also helped me study the way a powerful scene is developed. If you consider each hour installment as a chapter in your book, inspiration is rich in regards to character, motivation, growth arc, and themes. Next time you watch your favorite show, step back as a viewer and study the content like a writer.

REAL LIFE

My past dating disasters and close female friendships inspired my Searching For series. I had so many terrible dates that I laughed about years and years later. The series became a way to relate to all the readers who had gone through similar experiences. Taking disasters and spinning them with humor is a way to reach people.

In my book, *Everywhere and Every Way,* my heroine is getting ready for her date with the hero and is trying to find a way to make sure she doesn't sleep with him. She decides not to shave her legs as a way to curtail any intimate involvement. Imagine her horror when a kiss leads to more, and she realizes her mistake and is forced to confess her secret to the hero. I heard from many readers who identified with the scene, even though this famous feminine secret has now been outed.

QUOTES

Quotes from writing masters, religious leaders, or brilliant thinkers inspire me. If you've read any of my books, I always insert quotes that have made a difference in my life. Hearing words from someone else that strike a chord makes me feel part of a tribe, and therefore less alone. I've penned entire stories powered by the inspiration culled from a simple quote that struck me as a core belief of one potential hero or heroine.

When you hear a quote that inspires you, make sure to write it down in a journal or copy and paste it into a document that you go back to every now and again. You will be able to reference quotes that touch you for future blog posts, social media, and stories. I also use quotes to dig deeper into my character development. For instance, when I was creating my hero, Caleb, in *Everywhere and Every Way*, I picked a few quotes that would resonate with him. I did the same with his two brothers in the subsequent books, and the difference in what quotes affected them showed me the unique aspects of their personality.

PEOPLE

People inspire me every day. If you are involved in any type of group, sit back and watch the dynamics. You can see the leaders rise to the occasion, the reserved stay in the background, the social chatterer who keeps things lively, and the academic who is usually serious and on point. Of course, these are exaggerations and stereotypes, but you will be able to witness how personality types can become characters, and then you'll get a better idea of how to write their stories.

People's stories are important in the world of writing. My favorites are the underdogs. I love hearing about up-and-coming wiz kids who create their own companies with only their intelligence and a belief in what they are building. The boxer, who keeps getting up and finally wins the big fight. The bullied kid from school who becomes a billionaire CEO. The poverty stricken, who triumph and then decide to give back. I am always pondering these brief newsflashes on morning programs, local news, and social media. They're all stories in the making, as my muse sorts out the ones that will eventually stick, those that will appear on the page.

The rescue shelter I work with, Pets Alive, publicized a cry for help in social media featuring a beaten, abused pit bull whose back legs were paralyzed. The dog was about to be euthanized when workers from Pets Alive looked into his face and saw hope still burning bright in his eyes.

Even with all the pain he'd been through, he held onto the goodness of people. The shelter decided to save him.

His story went viral. Robert was finally adopted and fitted with a special scooter so he could get around. His owner created his own Facebook page, Rockin' Robert, and he has become a beloved public figure. Robert's story inspired me, and I knew I needed to write about it. I incorporated his story into my book, *Searching for Someday*, as my heroine's companion. I reached out to Robert's owner to interview him and find out about Robert, so that I could write his story as factually as possible. The love between Robert and my heroine in the book became as important as the primary love story between my heroine and the hero. I mingled the two stories to create a far-reaching theme that left readers more thoroughly satisfied. When my hero succumbed to Robert's charm, I knew the book had an extra layer that made all the difference.

I still receive e-mails regarding readers' love for Robert, and many have posted on Robert's Facebook page. Incorporating stories that inspire can help you write an extraordinary book.

THE INTERNET

The Internet can be very inspirational. Well, the good parts of the Internet—where there are lovely dog videos, people who rescue animals, real-life heroes who go out of their way to save others, and funny everyday people who want to make us happy—can be inspirational. These parts of the Internet remind me of the goodness in people and how one brave, kind act can topple a world that's sometimes too dark. It reminds us what it is to be human.

Taking some time to explore new websites and read articles helps bring fresh information to your stories. When I was writing the Searching For series, I investigated dating sites and matchmaking agencies, and became familiar with the social parameters of Match, eHarmony, and Tinder. Research has never been easier! Most answers are at the tips of our fingers.

MUSIC

Music is a part of my soul and an integral part of my writing. I always listen to music when I write; certain theme songs resonate with me. I have

write naked

created an entire novel based on one song that touches me deeply. Music is a passionate love in my life that goes hand-in-hand with my writing.

Many authors use playlists to set the mood of a book. In my self-published works, I've begun to include iTunes links at the back of my books so readers can easily purchase my playlist.

If you're struggling with your manuscript, try changing the music. Listening to specific songs while writing a sex scene or a fight scene can bring a burst of energy. If you write in silence, you may want to experiment with background sounds that boost creativity. There are wonderful sites that play soothing background sounds such as rainfall.

Open your senses to all possibilities in order to bring richness to your writing. Inspiration is the fuel that drives us forward as writers.

Fan this fire, allow it to burn hot and bright within you, and your days will be filled with stories.

Exercise

Write a list of everything that inspires you: people, books, movies, television, music, or any situation in your life. Anything and everything goes. Then study that list; allow yourself some precious time to ponder where you receive most of your inspiration. If you target something specific, make sure you honor your soul by giving yourself more of what inspires you.

16

the right to suck

"A blank piece of paper is God's way of telling us how hard it is to be God."

—SIDNEY SHELDON

I've read some brilliant writing books over the years, one being *Bird by Bird* by Anne Lamott. In it she talked about "shitty first drafts" and how important they are for the writing process.

Recently, I attended a Romance Writers of America conference and listened to the *New York Times* best-selling authors Susan Elizabeth Phillips and Jayne Ann Krentz talk about the things they regret in their writing careers. They opened up a big discussion about expectations: how writers have a million doubts when first committing the story to the page, and how the drone of negative voices can both stifle the creativity and the urge to write.

And then Susan said something brilliant: "I think we all need to have the right to suck."

Jayne quickly agreed, and I scribbled these words onto my notepad like it was a new Bible verse. I posted it on my computer. And I've never been the same since.

Now I have permission to suck.

When writers are creating and channeling God, we often don't feel like God. We mostly feel terrible. Like imposters. We fall under the crippling limitations of imposter syndrome, which I happen to also suffer from. No matter how hard I try, I never seem to be able to translate the greatness in my mind to the page. This fear of failure freezes the Muse until it becomes difficult to write anything. There's a wonderful quote from Julia Cameron in *The Artist's Way* that explains the perils of a career built on perfectionism:

> To the perfectionist, there is always room for improvement. The perfectionist calls this humility. In reality, it is egotism. It is pride that makes us want to write a perfect script, paint a perfect painting, perform a perfect audition monologue.
>
> Perfectionism is not a quest for the best. It is a pursuit of the worst in ourselves, the part that tells us that nothing we do will ever be good enough—that we should try again.
>
> No. We should not.

Sometimes when I write, all I can think of is the never-ending tirade of negative voices in my head that tell me even if my past books were good, this one will tank. I've written numerous books, but when this happens my mind goes blank. I can't remember how to plot, build a character, or write good dialogue. I rage inside, try desperately to put something on the page, and hate everything I write. It's a violent, painful, negative cycle of self-abuse that I've dealt with for years. Sometimes I feel like I've conquered both my fears and imposter syndrome, but then I'll find myself back at the computer, numb with fear, and realize it's still there. Like a poltergeist in a horror movie, the fear hides in the closet and pops out when I least expect it.

So, when I wrote the words, "permission to suck," on a shredded piece of paper, I was able to breathe. She was right. If I allow myself to suck for that first draft I can always fix it later. I can get help from my editor, agent, critique partners, or beta readers. When you're sketching out a story's skeleton, you must quiet the critics in your head and the ones whispering in your ear to just quit this stupid career because you're broke, tired, hungry, and it's gotten you nowhere.

Yeah, those voices.

Give yourself permission to *suck*.

Every day, I read that statement aloud. Well, not when I'm in editing mode, but editing is a different mind-set. When you're working on a first draft, you need to go crazy, reach for the stars, aspire for greatness, and allow yourself to fail spectacularly. *Through great suckage comes great writing.*

Believe me, I've harvested some of my words from these suckage sessions, words I believed were terrible. Guess what? I can pull together pieces here and there from these sessions to go into my works. If you're just pushing the words out the best you can instead of overthinking, the muse pokes her head out and says, "Hey, whatcha doin? Don't you need me?"

You ignore the muse because you're in suckage mode and don't really need her. But the muse is nosy, and pushy: "Let me see! I know I can help if you just get out of my way!" And she shoves at your shoulder, sees the words, and she's intrigued. Suddenly you're pouring great stuff onto the page because you allowed yourself to completely *suck*. Because if you know that what you're about to write is going to be completely horrible, there's no need to be scared. There are no voices warning you of expectations. There *are* no expectations. It's simply you, writing terribly, and you'll just fix your words later.

The best part? Many times you'll open your work and prepare to wince over yesterday's pages, but instead you find yourself pleasantly surprised. I've been known to shake my head and pat myself mentally on the back. I feel amazing. I feel like a superhero for a few seconds. Imagine that kind of talent. I thought my writing was terrible. Instead, it's great. If I actually tried to write something great, would that make my newest work Pulitzer Prize worthy?

Of course, at that moment, I've spiraled down because I've created expectations again. So I read my note and remind myself I can suck today, too.

Write it down. Post it. Allow yourself to believe it.

Then don't think too much and begin writing.

Now.

Exericse

If you read this chapter, you know what to do right now. Close the book while you're inspired to suck and go write something. Anything. Come back to this later.

17

the sewage and blockage of writing

"*Grandiose fantasies are a symptom of Resistance. They're the sign of an amateur. The professional has learned that success, like happiness, comes as a by-product of work. The professional concentrates on the work and allows rewards to come or not come, whatever they like.*"

—STEVEN PRESSFIELD, *THE WAR OF ART*

Let's talk writer's block.

When I was young and reading tons of craft books, I thought of writer's block as a mysterious badge of honor unique to "real" writers. It sounded … cool. I had this image of a gorgeous woman dressed in a trendy business suit, wearing glasses, holding her temples, and sitting at a messy desk with various papers, trying to make sense of all of her rich thoughts on writing.

First off, this image is completely wrong. I wear pajamas or yoga pants—anything without a zipper. I never look professional. And when writer's block is going on, there are no rich thoughts. It's just a barren wasteland where even cactuses are unwelcome; anyone who dares to visit dies a horrible, lonely death.

Not cool.

So I realized what writer's block truly was, experienced it myself, and accepted the term as part of the career. When people asked me how my book was going, I'd shake my head and tell them, "Writer's block." Even a layperson knows this term, thinking it's quite mysterious and deadly. I'd usually get an understanding nod. Sometimes I'd even receive an impressed look, which hitched up my all-important ego. People who don't know writers think we're exotic. Little do they know we live in solitary confinement, caught between the majestic highs of feeling like God and the lowest of lows of feeling like a mindless amoeba.

But flinging around the term "writer's block" made me feel validated.

I was trying to write. It wasn't my fault. I had writer's block.

Then I finally learned the real truth.

It really was all my fault.

If no writing is getting done, it doesn't matter what your excuse is, unless it's a tragedy. You have to write. Call it whatever you want, but somehow, someway, you have to get back to writing.

Eventually.

Before I approached writing as a full-time career, I suffered from writer's block for eight months. Eight. Months. I was writing a novella and had stalled out in chapter two. Every time I sat down to pick up where I left off, I went blank. I stared for hours. I wrote a word, then deleted it. I chewed my nails and lips. I spent endless time wondering why I couldn't see a purpose to my scenes. At that point it was an easy leap to convince myself I'd never sell the story anyway. Maybe I'd write something else. Maybe I'd take a much-needed break.

See, in my mind, I had no one waiting for it. No deadline. No eager reader. This can be a gift that allows creativity to fly. But it can also be the kiss of death.

Eight months later, I sat back down at the same scene. Without pause, I deleted the entirety of chapter two and started writing a brand-new scene.

write naked

I skipped the minutia and began again with action. I finished the book within the month, with no further issues to speak of.

Why? What happened that I could suddenly write again? It was a combination of things. First, I had no deadline, no agent, and no publisher lined up. When you are unpublished, you write the entire book first, then try to sell it. Therefore, I convinced myself it was easier to walk away. Even though I dealt with my own self-hatred at giving up, I rationalized that there was no valid reason to struggle through it. During those eight months, I took a hard look at my goals. My dream to be a successful writer was crumbling before me. If I didn't do the work, there'd be no story to sell. I went to an RWA conference in a last-ditch effort to see if I could turn my dream into a reality. I networked, listened to best-selling authors, and took classes. Over and over again, I heard the same thing: A writing career is unique. You can study craft and network and be inspired. But the hard stuff is done completely alone. You have to write. You cannot run away from yourself. It's you in a room with a blank page and a closet full of your own personal monsters. Nothing can prepare you for that, no matter how many books or classes you take.

When I made it home from the RWA conference, I committed myself to finishing that story, no matter what. When I sat in front of that scene that left me helplessly rooted in a tangle of nothingness, I resorted to my only option. I deleted the entire chapter. I restarted at a good part, one that interested me. I realized that for the past eight months I'd tried too hard to involve my heroine in a witty, sparkling conversation with a secondary character. I tried so hard that I'd bored myself.

A lot of blockage takes place because you're writing a scene that isn't important. In such cases, it's best to skip over the boring stuff and come back to it later. Follow the story in the beginning, because messing with minute details can kill the fun. Of course, maybe you enjoy writing details, and then maybe you get blocked at a sex scene or with dialogue. Whatever the case, when you find yourself blocked, mark that spot with a bunch of XXXs and start again at a point that is fun or interesting. Because if you're bored writing it, I can guarantee readers will be bored reading it.

THE DECONSTRUCTION OF WRITER'S BLOCK

Writer's block happens in different ways and at various stages in a writer's career. It's important to recognize where you are in order to understand your specific block.

Of course, as a young writer, I also realized that I was firmly in a writer's playground, just playing with words. There's much less blockage when you've bashed through to your subconscious and simply don't care. No one's telling you the book has to hit a list, that you need to pay bills, or that your writing is absolute crap. You sit down, ignore the negative Nellys trolling your space, and create. You find out who you are. You pour all those pumping hormones and big ideas into the story. You are full of possibility and the prospect of a rich, full life of potential beats with every tap of the keys.

But in a full-time, day-to-day writing career, writer's block is probably going to happen. Actually, writer's block can happen for anyone who's thinking of diving into a book. Or it can happen to someone who's just started, but she doesn't know what she's gotten into. That's a scary feeling. It's like you thought you played a Jedi mind trick on your muse, but really, your muse fooled you. You thought you were safe at chapter three. You were so wrong.

I've dealt with writer's block in a variety of ways, depending on the circumstance or project. Each time I did, my decision on how to deal with it became a huge turning point for me in my career. Sometimes blockage is helpful to get you to that next level of writing. The problem is the connotation of writer's block. Blockage gives me the impression I'm completely stuck, and it will take large pieces of machinery to blast through.

Sewage, on the other hand, makes me think of an obstacle I can get through. Sewage can be worked with. But too much sewage causes blockage.

Take care of the sewage first, and you will no longer be blocked.

From now on, think of writer's block as sewage—a temporary backup that will eventually clear. It's weird, yes. But changing words changes meanings, and as writers, we all know how important thoughts are when implementing action.

Sewage

Sewage is the type of backup you hope your house will never have so you don't have to call the big truck with a *pooper scoopers* logo on the side. Think of it as a black, pulpy, smelly mass that jams up the creativity pipes. You try to get excited about a project or a scene, and you sit down and get … nothing. Or, perhaps worse, you begin to question your motivation for starting or continuing the project. Suddenly, what seemed exciting and fresh is now stale and unappealing.

Some of the sewage I've encountered includes negative thoughts, the influence of outsiders, expectations, life events, and burnout. These are nasty little things that can block up your creativity pipe fast. Let's break each one down and discuss.

Negative Thoughts

We all have them, because we're human. It's harder than we think to attack a creative project without doubts or negative thoughts dogging us each step of the way. I started suppressing these thoughts deep inside, where I thought they wouldn't bother me, because I just needed to get on with the process of writing. It worked and I was able to continue working for a while, avoiding all negative thoughts and busting through my book. Eventually, though, the sewage jammed up and there were too many negative things inside, blocking up my creative soul.

See, I never dealt with the negative thoughts. I avoided them. And if you don't deal with negative thoughts, they'll eventually come spewing out of you in one full swoop, like the *Goosebumps* movie where all the monsters jumped from the books at once.

Scary. Creepy. *Gross.*

At first, I tried to ignore the monsters, but I couldn't seem to write. I realized I had to do something to counteract the damaging thoughts. I used a technique called "morning pages," from Julia Cameron's *The Artist's Way.*

The exercise is simple: You rise each morning and immediately write three pages—longhand—without stopping. You do not stop. Ideally, when you finish, you've dumped all the nagging thoughts onto the page. This technique allows you to free your mind from negativity and get to work.

When I was working a full-time day job, I couldn't get into the practice of writing when I first woke up. I had kids to get ready and a long commute, so I wrote my three pages on my morning break. Instead of socializing, I'd lock myself away and write. When I returned to my story that evening, I found I'd quieted the negative voices because I'd given them an outlet instead of keeping them trapped in my head.

If you're groaning right now, because you hate the idea of having to write three additional pages, I understand. Just give it a try. It not only worked for me, but the process helped me discover amazing things about my life. I found my way out of my day job and into one that suited me better until I could write full-time. In my morning pages, I wrote out all my emotionally abusive boyfriends, and explored the most important traits I needed for a long-term, happy relationship. And if you've read either the Marriage to a Billionaire or Searching For series, you know I use a written love spell for my characters in their search for a soul mate. This idea was born directly from my morning pages.

Rereading my pages, I discovered that I'd written my way to a better path. I have always believed in the power of words. Why would I doubt the power of committing words to the page? By releasing my positive intentions and negative thoughts, I'd freed myself from the sewage. And by using morning pages, you'll be able to do the same.

The Influence of Outsiders

This one is tough, especially if you're a people pleaser, like me. The idea that people I knew were thinking negative things about me drove me crazy. I needed everyone to like me. I craved support and excitement behind my decision to write.

When I was young, a lot of positivity in my life surrounded my writing. My mother never discouraged me, and we were a family who always loved to read. Friends and family thought my decision to write was exciting and different. Teachers and mentors praised me along the way. I consider myself lucky to have that foundation of support. My first real obstacle was an English teacher in the honors program.

I was in junior high school at the time and still interested in pursuing a writing career. Throughout the year, our teacher would have us write essays on various classics, such as *Huckleberry Finn* and *Othello*, then read them aloud to the class. I worked hard on them, and each time I stood up to read, she berated me. She criticized me in front of my peers. Made faces *while I was reading*.

By the end of the year, my confidence had shriveled. My stomach ached each time I went to class. On the last day, she came around to speak to each of us and offer a personal good-bye. Stopping at my desk, she told me something that has become a big part of who I was and who I am today.

"I don't think an honors English class is in your best interest next year," she said with a smug grin. "You're struggling. You don't really belong here."

"But I want to be a writer," I whispered.

She paused. "I don't know if that's a good idea," she finally said. I detected a flash of triumph in her eyes. As a quiet, introverted student, I remember being completely shocked at both her words and attitude. The bell rang, and I walked out of her class for the final time, stunned.

She haunted me afterward for a long, long time.

I went home and pondered her words. She was an honors English teacher. She knew good writing. I was just a teenager. I didn't know good writing. If she told me I would never be a writer, she must be right.

It was a dark time for me. I felt as if I needed to make an important decision about my life. I didn't want to be a bad writer. If I didn't have the talent, I convinced myself it would be best to let my dream go and not torture myself for the rest of my life. I could find something else that would interest me. Maybe incorporate a part of writing in a new career to help satisfy my soul.

Maybe teach.

Very quietly, one night, I decided to quit writing. I'd listen to someone who knew best and try very hard to make peace with the truth.

Writing this still makes me choke up. I think of all the kids out there who love to write, paint, or sing—whatever it is—and I think about all the misguided adults who advise them about "real life," in an attempt to *help* them. Meanwhile, they destroy the very flicker of light that makes life worth living. They destroy the artistic soul, already struggling to live in the face of a proper, monetary, civilized world.

Looking back, I know I faced a road with two paths. Perhaps if I'd taken the other route, my life would have been different. I'm not even sure what made me believe in myself that much at such a young age, but

I refused to go down without a fight. There was something inside me that screamed "Don't give up!" It told me not to believe in her, but to believe in myself.

It took me a while, but I started writing again. Her words still lingered, but I buried them deeper with each strike of the keyboard. I burned for revenge. I believed one day, when my books were in print, or my byline appeared in a magazine, she would see it and be shocked. She became my own personal nemesis; she gave me drive to prove her wrong.

The best way to overcome other people's negative opinions or feedback is simple: Decide to prove them wrong. If someone tells you your writing is bad, keep writing and get better. If someone tells you you'll never make a living by writing, research what you need to do to pay the bills. Create a positive action to combat every negative thought. You need to make a conscious choice to combat all the things that drain your writing energy, and you can do that by completing two tasks:

Write.

Commit.

Most of the people telling you it's impossible are the ones who either failed or quit.

And the reason they failed is because they quit after failing the first time. Or the second. You, though, will not quit whether it's your first failure or fiftieth. Therefore, you will succeed.

I've failed over and over again, sometimes in spectacular glory, in both love and work. My greatest accomplishments are the ones where I bashed my head against the brick wall, got up, and tried again.

Think Rocky Balboa, and when you do, remember what he said: "It ain't about how hard you hit. It's about how hard you can get hit and keep moving forward; how much you can take and keep moving forward."

How do you get those wormlike negative voices out of your brain so you can write and not get blocked?

Think about what will really happen if you fail. Will you die? Probably not. Will you be embarrassed or humiliated? Maybe. Will you lose money or time? Maybe. Will you regret trying?

No.

write naked

Sift through the negative and make a conscious decision to combat it with action.

Write. Commit.

Soon, the voices in your head will quiet, and you'll see only what's ahead of you.

Expectations

When writers begin, they always start simply.

You have a story to tell. Usually, you're driven to write it, because the voices of the story talk to you. You feel as if you are living in dual worlds—your imagination and real life. When you sit down to tell your story, your vision, and the way the story is revealed, triumphs over all. Nothing gets in your way. Sitting down to write a story is a purity of consciousness so heartbreakingly beautiful and fragile, writers seek it like a drug—endlessly going back for one quick hit, hoping they'll feel it just one more time.

Writing without expectations is completely freeing and takes place in the subconscious.

Writing with expectations limits the writer and the ability to tell the story.

Let me give you an example. When I first wrote my book, *The Marriage Bargain*, it was before I had made a name for myself. I'd published a few things and cultivated an extremely small following. I wrote the book without expectations, following the story and throwing my entire soul into it. Emotion dripped from the page, because I'd cut and bled to give my characters breath.

When I finally sold the book many years later, I was shocked when it went viral. At that point, I began writing the second book in the series. I was excited for it, and still having fun in the writer's playground. But once *The Marriage Bargain* became a worldwide bestseller, and publishers were asking to buy it, and everyone was frantically anticipating its follow-up, the second book stalled.

Day after day, I froze at my keyboard. Fear rattled inside of me—I was concerned over the expectations of how the second book would live up to the first. My publishers wanted lightning to strike twice. I doubted my initial instincts and tried to see if I could make it as funny, heartfelt, and big as the first one.

If I didn't, it would be a failure, in my mind. I'd disappoint readers, my publishers, and my editor. I'd be a hack. A one-hit wonder. Readers would never buy another book from me, and my career would end.

I learned some very hard lessons during this period, lessons I still fall back on. As I lost sleep and my deadline approached, I'd face that blank page and feel complete frustration. How had I made *The Marriage Bargain* a perfect book? How could I make *this* book a bestseller, too?

My answer was brutal but it was the truth. I couldn't. I couldn't reach deep enough to make this book like the first. I had to accept that I would *never* write another book like *The Marriage Bargain*. It was a different story, written at a different point of my life. To write a cookie-cutter story just to compare it to the breakout success of the first would be cheating. A lie.

I knew I had to write my new book, and in order to do so, I needed to "clear the mechanism"—a popular saying from the movie, *For The Love of the Game*. The movie revolves around a famous baseball pitcher, portrayed by Kevin Costner. As he settles in for an inning, the roars and loud noise from the crowd begin to affect his pitching. He repeats the mantra, "clear the mechanism," and slowly, the sounds of the crowd settle to silence, and he is able to concentrate on his work.

I cleared the mechanism. I quieted the outside sounds and focused on the voice of my characters. My *new* characters. Characters who were nothing like the ones who had charmed the world in the previous book.

Unfortunately I was told that my new heroine was a bit bitchy. And my hero wasn't as well liked.

But I was also told that one of my new secondary characters, Mama Conte, was brilliant and would steal reader's hearts in future books.

I was told a scene where my heroine tries to cook homemade pasta in Italy was hysterical.

I remember my editor telling me she loved the second book even more than the first, but she didn't know if it would sell as well. We both weren't even sure why. All we knew was this book, *The Marriage Trap*, was different. But, it still contained my trademark stamp—my voice. My stories are so steeped in voice that readers can quickly identify my work, whether they like it or not.

Expectations can stifle your creative voice and confine you to a blank page. Dragging these expectations to the forefront and examining them is a good tool for fighting back. Give expectations light and they eventually wither. Feed them secretly in the dark and they grow until they devour you whole.

The Marriage Trap never sold as well as *The Marriage Bargain*, though sales were still solid. But I still love that book. And I learned a lesson I'd repeat over and over in my career.

We must accept that every book will be different. We must give each of our stories space to grow and time to flourish. Treat each story as a unique individual. Some books will do better than others. You might hate writing some books, but you'll love writing others. Let's leave expectations to the readers and publishers and keep our creativity for ourselves.

There is only one thing I judge each of my books by. Did I do everything in my power to write the best story possible *at that time*?

If the answer is yes, then it's out of my hands whether the book sells or tanks. I did my best. Let that be your expectation for your own work. Everything else will simply block your progress.

Life Events

Life has the ability to deliver some painful punches. We lose people we love. We lose animals we love. We struggle with our children's ups and downs. We worry about finances. We deal with divorce. There are so many stressful and heartbreaking events that knock us off our feet and distract us from writing. Sometimes life makes it hard to believe we will ever find joy again in writing.

I remember when my father was going through a major surgery to remove a cancerous, basketball-sized tumor in his stomach. At the time, my self-published novella, *Beyond Me*, was being released, and I was on deadline with Simon & Schuster for *Searching for You*.

I was warned the operation was risky, and his chance to survive wasn't good. Carrying this burden, my family waited through a fifteen-hour surgery, relieved when he survived the operation.

But he had a long road ahead and needed to be watched carefully. I spent a week away from home so I could be near the hospital, and I worked on my laptop when I could. My father began to get better. He was eventually released (in record time, it turns out) and his case is still highly documented as a huge success—and a tiny bit of a miracle.

Awesome. I scurried home, finished up the novella, and sent it out.

My editor called me back and said it was a disaster.

Yep. I knew it was.

I remember her asking me what had happened. When I reminded her of my father's surgery, she completely understood—it was a lightbulb moment for her. She told me to take another month off and heal a bit, let the story simmer. She forwarded me her edits and suggestions, and I took my time diving back in. After revising and returning it to her, she proclaimed it "perfect," sending it straight to the copy editor.

Sometimes we need time to breathe, to heal. We need to accept and acknowledge that our emotional capacity is full, that there is no more room available. Not even for a book.

I know that's difficult with deadlines. I know writers who struggle with constant injuries and pain, yet manage to write their way through. But if you don't have any juice left, if your book is dull and lifeless, you may need to step away from the page for a while.

Yes, writing is important. But so is your emotional health. Sometimes you need to just be where you are and take a necessary break. This will allow you some fresh air, and when you need to write again, you'll have fewer ghosts to battle.

If you're reaching a limit where you haven't been able to get back to work, you need to ease your muse back into the game. Write in your journal. Write an essay about your experience. When I lost my beloved dog, it took me a while to write again, and I channeled most of my grief by writing an essay about him. I documented his sweet personality, his goofy grin, and the way he managed to plunk himself down into the middle of any situation with the stubbornness of a donkey. And I cried a lot while I was writing.

Writing can help ease the pain, but you need to remove it from any expectations.

Let your gift of writing begin to heal your soul. Writing doesn't always have to be about a reader. It can also be just for you.

Burnout

Sometimes the presence of sewage is a warning sign to slow down and refill the well. Maybe you need to find a new way to approach your story. Or change a POV, or delete a scene. There's nothing wrong with taking a drive, a walk, or a shower to connect with your creativity. (It's when you find you've driven into the next state, without your laptop to write, that you have a real problem.)

A break is not giving in to writer's block. Today's writers are being encouraged to produce more work than ever before. Many writers have gone the hybrid route—publishing both traditionally and independently—and they constantly need to write a new project in between contracts. Writers are told they need to produce new material in order to keep their work in the spotlight. Between blogs, promotion, social media, and works-in-progress, burnout is a valid way to run into writer's block.

If you think burnout is affecting your ability to write, you need to carefully examine your life and current business plan. Because you cannot sacrifice quality in the quest for quantity. If the quality of your writing suffers, readers will eventually wise up and stop buying your books. You are the quality gatekeeper, more so than any editor or publicist. You control the quality of your books. If you're burnt out, you've lost something essential to your career as a writer. I advise a three-pronged approach to work your way through it:

1. **GET OFF SOCIAL MEDIA AND THE INTERNET.** You need to protect your creative energy. The Internet drains it. You need to encourage your muse to come back out to play. Turn off any of these distractions—it's critical.
2. **DO FUN THINGS.** Watch a show. See a play. Take a hike. Go horseback riding. Cook a three-course meal. Break from your work so you can come back in a fresh state of mind.
3. **REDO YOUR CALENDAR.** Be brutal. It's time to cut off any activity that is draining you. Ask for help with responsibilities around the house. Cancel engagements that you used to enjoy but now dread. You may

even need to cancel a conference or speaking engagement in order to take charge of your writing again. Start using that red pen and slash away at commitments that are sucking the life from your soul.

Then write. Begin with a scene that interests you or start a whole new chapter just for the importance of starting with a new page. Play a bit. Do some freewriting. Once you get into it, it'll be easier to keep going.

Try setting a timer. Commit to half an hour with your butt firmly in a chair, and don't move. Not even to use the bathroom. Certainly not for that cup of coffee you *think* you need or the quick check of someone's Facebook status. Eventually you'll write something even if it's *This is the dumbest exercise Jennifer Probst made me do.*

One word always leads to another.

If you don't tend to burn out, eventually it will come back in the form of long-term writer's block. If you aren't writing what you want, consider it a wake-up call. Maybe it's time to look at what you *crave* to write. Sometimes sewage is a way to make you pay attention—a path to growth and change. What made you happy a few years ago may be strangling you alive today. You owe it to yourself and your readers to be true to who you are, to write the stories that emanate from your soul.

That's why calendars are important. Take the time to calculate what your contract responsibilities are, where you want to go with your writing career, and what your new goals are.

I know a writer who was well known for erotic fiction. She wrote in the genre for years and was quite successful. But she eventually realized she didn't want to write erotic fiction any longer. She experienced a change in her lifestyle and longed to write Christian romance. That's a *big* departure from her original work. But she knew it had to be done, or she'd suffer personally.

If we force ourselves to keep to the status quo, if we refuse change, we cheat everyone including our readers. The woman I described above made a long-term business plan, changed her website, networked with new contacts, and began writing what she needed to write.

Another author well-known for her dark romance decided she needed a break. She published a romantic comedy and was quite open about expectations of her readers. She explained she'd been in a dark place for a while and needed to let some light in. The story poured from her soul and helped her heal. She'd written the book for herself and didn't expect great sales, but was proud of the result and happy to share it with the world.

The book ended up hitting a best-seller list. Afterward, she was able to dive back into the books suited to her brand. Sometimes we need to take a creative risk for ourselves to combat sewage.

Deadlines

I've learned another important thing about writer's block. If you give into it and its connotations, you may stop writing. I've realized sometimes I'm better off working within the constraints of a tight deadline. When my muse has too much time before a delivery date, she likes to play. She has affairs with other story ideas, and becomes stubbornly slow or silent when I try to get ahead. Sometimes I'm firm with her and force her to focus and produce words. Other times I let her lead, and I give in to that impulse to catch up on the latest show or book. I go shopping. I do errands. Then I realize I have to complete thirty-five thousand words in ten days.

Yeah, that's happened. Actually, a month before writing this chapter, I completed thirty-five thousand words in ten days. I experienced a bad case of sewage and spent too much time giving in to it rather than pushing through. When I realized I had to deliver my manuscript—I was too proud to ask for an extension—I had a complete breakdown and locked myself in my office for two weeks. It was an ugly experience. My fear held me in a grip of sleepless terror. What if the book sucked? How did I rush through the job without sacrificing quality?

Forcing myself to face that particular book with no other escape route helped me focus. I ate and breathed that book. When I stumbled from my office in a blur, my poor kids looked at me like I'd arrived from Mars. I slowly found the story by removing every other distraction in my life. The beginning was brutal. I sat for hours, forcing terrible words that didn't flow, onto that blank page. I slowly found the threads, hung on for dear life, and followed them. Halfway through, it stopped sucking. When I finished, I was able to go back and rewrite the first half, because I now knew the story.

In that case, I didn't have time to indulge in writer's block. Oh, sure it existed in my mind, but it no longer mattered. I was on deadline and needed to deliver a book in order to eat. I had plenty of time and squandered it. I suffered the punishment.

Sounds fair to me.

Old-fashioned stubbornness, perseverance, and pride sometimes work just fine.

Ass in the chair until you find your story works just fine.

I read a fascinating article titled "Writer's Block and Its History" in *The New Yorker*. The article explores how various groups of writers experienced blockage, and the underlying emotional element that existed in all of the groups. Sometimes, in the pursuit for productive work, we forget the importance of understanding our humanity. Emotion in all forms—from anger, depression, or lack of interest—affect our daily life and can block us from being creatively happy. The article goes on to state the top four causes of block seemed to revolve around: perfectionism, comparison to others work, lack of creative freedom, and external validation factors.

Researchers learned the closest thing to a cure was when writers allowed for error, trusted the process, and embraced creative work in all forms.

Seems the muse doesn't flourish with too many rules for too long.

I've included the link to the article here for your reading pleasure: *http://www.newyorker.com/science/maria-konnikova/how-to-beat-writers-block*.

··*Exercise*·································

Think about the last time you felt blocked in your writing. Did you have a method to get through it? What did you learn from it? Are you experiencing writer's block more often than you used to, or was that episode isolated to a particular project? Learning about your triggers and habits in writing is helpful. Analyzing your behavior and how you respond to sewage is important in understanding the triggers that cause blockage. Write down your thoughts and keep them in a safe place to read later.

18

the right hook and warm-up jabs

"There is something delicious about writing the first words of a story. You'll never quite know where they'll take you."

—BEATRIX POTTER

Hooks are critical to a book on many levels. A hook is what draws the reader in and keeps them there. It's the premise. It's a promise to the reader. It allows for the all-important impulse buy. It demands the reader keep flipping pages until they reach the end.

A book bought is a beautiful thing.

A book read is a holy thing.

When you deliver on a hook, you satisfy a reader. That means they'll buy more of your books. It's also important in this era of marketing and promotion. Hooks were one of the elements picked by best-selling authors as a trademark secret to keep hitting best-seller lists. By deconstructing the power of a hook, we can see how it affects readers and propels them forward.

Jabs are also important in keeping the story moving. A jab warms up the reader for the all-important right hook. Together, a book is stronger when combining these two elements.

Let's compare a book to a boxing match. As I've seen every Rocky movie multiple times, along with *Cinderella Man*, *The Champ*, and *Southpaw*, I think I'm qualified to use this metaphor. We'll name one boxer the protagonist and the other the antagonist. No boxer comes out with the knockout punch. That would just be stupid. Instead, they begin with warm-up jabs, dancing on their feet, and experimenting with punches so they get an idea of the opponent's strengths and weaknesses.

The audience knows and anticipates such foreplay. They are usually patient enough to allow the two opponents to find their ground and build their offense and defense.

Now, if nothing ever happened except dancing and minor jabs, the audience would boo. They'd get angry. They bought tickets to watch action and drama, and to root for the underdog or the champion. They have an emotional investment in that boxing ring, and there's no satisfaction if they don't get what they paid for.

Finally, the audience holds their breath as the punches increase. The antagonist lands a wicked jab. Then another. Blood flows, and the protagonist stumbles, weakening under the attack. But the protagonist refuses to go down. Spying an opening, and, in a whirling flash, the protagonist pulls back his arm and lets the right hook fly. Bones crack, and the antagonist staggers back.

The audience roars. They want more. Always more.

The final punch is usually a thing of grace and beauty. Whipped into a frenzy, the crowd waits for the knockout punch. And when they get it, they are finally happy, because the antagonist is the one lying beaten on the ground.

Think of your book as a boxing match. As an unknown author, you're asking the reader to take a chance on your book (more so than an author the reader already knows and likes). Your hook is clearly alluded to in your packaging. The title, the book jacket blurb, the cover art. The reader pauses to consider these things before making a decision to buy a book.

write naked

Maybe there's an author blurb that is intriguing. A few reviews written by authors she knows. Maybe the cover art caught her attention.

She flips to the first page, scans the words. Whether you open with a gunshot, a sex scene, or a quiet reflection from the character, it doesn't matter. That first page must hook the reader. It must make him want to keep reading, to flip to the next page.

What kind of writing does that?

Action. Or conflict. Rip away your character's security on the first page and send her spiraling.

Or tease the reader with wispy words of description and thought that immediately tie him to the character, urging him to find out more.

Use emotional scenes to grab and take hold.

It simply doesn't matter where you want to begin as long as it's *interesting*. What makes writing interesting? Emotion. Intrigue. Can you back up the promise that your blurb and title make right away, on page one? That's even better.

My novel *Searching for Always* pits a cynical alpha cop against a Zen yoga instructor.

My opening line: *Officer Stone Petty was having a shit day.*

My reader immediately knows my hero will be rough around the edges. The tone of voice sets the stage and pulls the reader into his crappy day. We are grounded in his profession, his voice, and his thoughts. And I've made a promise concerning what my reader should expect right away, on page one. I continue to bait the reader with mini hooks throughout the chapters, pulling them toward the finish.

Here are some more examples of first lines:

> Daisy Devreaux had forgotten her bridegroom's name.
> —Susan Elizabeth Phillips, *Kiss An Angel*

This is a marriage of convenience that sets the stage with a quick hook.

> It wasn't a very likely place for disappearances, at least at first glance.
> —Diana Gabaldon, *Outlander*

This is an epic, historical adventure waiting to be unveiled with the mysterious hook.

> When the sun dipped low in the sky, dripping the last of its fire, the children huddled together to hear the next part of the tale.
>
> —Nora Roberts, *Dance of the Gods*

This is the promise of an epic tale. A reader holds her breath from the very first line, waiting.

> I was born beautiful.
>
> —Emily Giffin, *Something Blue*

This first line sets up our relationship with the heroine—we are promised to love and hate her, and we're immediately intrigued.

Each of these first lines is masterfully crafted to promote the promised hook. Plant quick jabs in each chapter to keep the storytelling sharp and compel readers to continue. This includes teasing the reader with a secret, or dropping a fascinating revelation about a character, or setting the stage for conflict. A boxer needs to keep moving and dancing to avoid punches. This is when you give your story the necessary breathing room. When your reader is once again soothed, keep her off balance by a surprise uppercut—send them down a false road, throw in a blistering love scene, or force your character to experience some uncomfortable growth. When your reader is holding her breath, turning the pages, it's time for big action.

Hit her with the right hook.

This is not the ending. It's the black moment—the crescendo of conflict where your hero and heroine break up, are forced apart, or begin to doubt the future of their relationship. It may be simple, but it must be epic. You must convince the reader that there is no hope, though the reader is promised a happily-ever-after. The book will be a safe place for a reader to experience all the messy, raw emotions of relationships.

Make sure you strip away every last barrier to your hero or heroine. Leave them naked and bleeding, walking in front of a crowd of strangers. Think of Queen Cersei's epic scene in *A Game of Thrones*.

The arrogant Queen, who viewers love to hate, is sentenced to prison for sins against the Church. She refuses to yield but eventually realizes she must be free in order to help her son, the King, who is back at home in the castle. She decides to take the deal the Church offers in exchange for release: She must atone for her sins.

First the Queen is dragged outside and stripped of her clothes. Her long hair is shorn off, and she is shoved into the streets, forced to walk the long roads leading back to the castle. Massive crowds line the roads— shouting, throwing rocks, and insulting her in vicious fashion. The surging chant of "Shame!" fills the air. Her feet and naked body are bloodied, and humiliation is etched permanently in her psyche as she walks for what seems like hours to both the Queen and the audience.

Every viewer squirms with discomfort at the degradation and vulnerability she suffers. Though she is evil, the writer is able to construct a scene in which we feel sorry for her. He has built a character rich with layers. Queen Cersei is both interesting and dynamic.

Give that same depth to your characters. Then put her in a point of no return situation.

Then fix it.

Then save her.

Let's take my book, *Searching for Always*, and break down the boxing match.

I showed you the first line of the hook. My hero is eventually mandated to attend anger management classes, where my heroine is the teacher. Though they're complete opposites, they're attracted to one another. Stone is also holding back a secret about his past that my heroine is trying to uncover in order to help him deal with anger issues.

After the hook, I present a series of sharp jabs. This scene takes place during a counseling session that dredges up a painful event for my hero, keeping the reader engaged to learn the truth.

> "You think I'm a chump asking these questions. You think I'm easily manipulated," she said.
>
> "I never said any of those things."
>
> "Didn't have to. Who else were you protecting?"
>
> He blinked. "Just told you. Me. My mother."
>
> Her voice softened, deepening to a velvety, soothing itch, urging him to spill all his secrets. "I think there's someone else. Another person in the house. A foster brother or sister? A friend? You got used to dealing with your

father's rage until he went after someone new." She leaned forward, gaze locked on him with a sense of urgency. Within those emerald depths lay a vastness of understanding and gentleness he'd never been on the receiving end of. "Who was it, Stone?"

He jerked back. He'd gotten bashed in the face with a baseball bat and refused to cry. There was so much inside scarred up and dead he was grateful he never had to revisit. But Arilyn's final question stole his breath and drew blood.

He was done.

Stone stood up. "This is bullshit," he stated quietly. "I told you before I'll be straight with you, but don't dick around in my head and think you won't get hurt."

She never flinched. Just studied him for a long time, their gazes locked in a battle, until she slowly nodded. "I apologize. I went too deep, too fast. Why don't you sit back down and we'll talk about something else."

Who did she think she was? A yoga teacher turned matchmaker playing at being a therapist? She led a charmed life and had no idea of the harsh realities in the world. She controlled her reality while she viewed others through a set of rosy glasses so she could avoid the true mess. Breathing. Meditating. Helping animals. Even with a broken relationship behind her, she pretended to understand and transcend, citing a higher purpose and acceptance she didn't really feel.

It was a bunch of crap.

Maybe it was time she knew what it felt like to have her safe bubble ripped away.

This jab was critical in hinting at Stone's secret, and developing another layer of conflict within their relationship. Stone Petty believes he is not worthy of a strong, healthy relationship. I continue jabbing the reader, leading up to the right hook, a scene where Stone breaks up with the heroine, and gives away Pinky, the rescue dog he's fallen in love with—a dog who's gone through hell and back, who's started to love and trust again. It was a double rejection, and I had a hard time writing it. Stone had screwed up big time and betrayed the ones who loved him. Here's a peek:

"Come to bed with me."

The invitation was more than physical. It was an askance of the next step for them both.

Stone pulled back and stared at her beautiful face. Stroked her swollen lips. Cupped her cheeks. Kissed her again.

"I can't Arilyn. I can't do this."

Pain and grief flickered in those green eyes. "You can. You're choosing not to try."

"I'm choosing not to disappoint you. It's better this way. You're better off without me."

She pushed him away and he let her. He got himself together and when he came back, she was frozen in place, her arms wrapped around her chest, squeezing tight, as if desperate for warmth. Something broke inside of him and Stone realized he'd never be whole again. Still, he didn't reach for her.

He believed he was doing the right thing. Better now than later. Better now before it was too much for both of them.

He stopped at the door. "I'll bring Pinky over in the morning."

Her words were cold and deliberate. "Don't. I'm asking you to keep her, Stone. You don't have to be there for me. I've learned I'm strong and can heal. But Pinky needs to believe in something, and for now, that's you. If you let her go, you'll break her heart. And she may not heal from that."

His eyes burned as he reached for the knob. "I'll think about it."

I deliver two right hooks back to back in this book. In the next scene, Stone decides to give the dog back, and the break with Arilyn is final. Pinky's pitiful whines as he leaves haunt the reader. This is where everything has been lost. You must pull every safety net from the reader and leave her devastated. This is the only way your final knockout becomes an epic moment.

When he finally realizes he's been a total asshole and tries to get both Pinky and Arilyn back, the heroine turns him away. The rescue dog has been returned to the shelter, so it won't be easy for him to fix things. In a showdown with the animal shelter manager, he finally gets the dog back and is forgiven. He shows up with Pinky and begs Arilyn's forgiveness. Because the dog was strong enough to forgive Stone, the heroine decides to give him another chance.

You must leave readers reeling with the right hook. Every jab leads up to the black moment.

Make it a knockout, and win the match.

You'll gain a reader for life.

Take the story you're working on and examine the black moment. Check for jabs, and the all-important right hook. Is it powerful enough? Can you pump up the intensity? Add more jabs throughout your chapter? Leave ending hooks or sentences at the end of every chapter?

Perform a thorough analysis and try to write at least one revision that makes the black moment more important to your reader.

building characters

"*Elderly people are not always craggy, wrinkled, stooped over, forgetful, or wise. Teenagers are not necessarily rebellious, querulous, or pimple-faced. Babies aren't always angelic, or even cute. Drunks don't always slur their words. Characters aren't types. When creating a character, it's essential to avoid the predictable. Just as in language we must beware of clichés. When it comes to character, we are looking for what is true, what is not always so, what makes a character unique, nuanced, indelible.*"

—DANI SHAPIRO, *STILL WRITING*

Characters ranked as one of the top trademark secrets of best-selling authors. There's a reason for that, and it's the same reason this subject of craft is continuously offered in workshops all over the world. I believe creating strong, memorable characters is the key to making a successful book that leaves an impression on a reader. I also think there are certain ways to create characters that feel lifelike to readers.

When I begin a new romance novel, the first thing I do is think about my characters. My goal is to go beyond the physical description, character history, and basic personality in making sure each character breathes air. I need to identify with them. I need them to have annoying habits, to screw up, and to show the reader that they will never be perfect but they're still doing their best.

These are the types of characters readers want to follow on a journey. A book can have the most exotic setting, the most thrilling plot, the deepest theme, but if the reader doesn't care about the characters, the entire book will fall flat.

The skill set required for the challenge will change, too, depending on what type of romance (or, any genre) you are writing. For instance, when I write category-type romance novels of around 55,000 words, I need to draw my characters quickly and sharply in order to get the reader on board in a more compact story. I have less time to linger on secondary characters or spend pages on details.

Same thing with novellas. The characters have to come alive within a few brushstrokes, and they need to be lean and mean. A writer's job is to relate the most important qualities that make a character unique. The best way to do this is to throw the character into a situation and watch how he reacts.

Everyone has heard the famous writers mantra, "Show, don't tell." That means write active, not passive.

With shorter books, these components are even more critical. Readers need to identify with your hero or heroine in the first few pages. Instead of rambling about your hero's fear of commitment, open your book with him breaking off a relationship or scoffing at his friend's engagement. Don't tell the reader he's a workaholic. Show him at the police station, drinking stale coffee at 2 a.m., pondering why he doesn't have a life.

In my novel *Searching for Perfect*, I'd originally opened with a lengthy introduction to my hero—a rocket scientist, nerd, and social misfit—desperate to find a woman to settle down with and marry. I thought it was quite clever until my editor reminded me he wasn't doing anything. He was just reflecting about these qualities, which became a big tell-fest. *Boring*. I fixed it by grounding him in a real-life situation: a speed-dating event where he showed his awkwardness, sporting orange skin from a self-tanner gone wrong and bombing out on every meet and greet. Here's an example. In this scene, my hero, Ned, is frustrated at his past speed-dating encounters and decides to get right to the point.

Ding.

By the time he hit table twenty, he was aggravated, tired, thirsty, and disillusioned. Most cared about his appearance, money, or man toys, and all he wanted to do was get serious and leave all the junk behind. Despite weeks of reading women's magazines, he'd flunked every five-minute session.

Finally, he reached the last date. The woman seemed nice enough, but he'd been here before. No more. This time, he was running the date his way.

"Hi, I'm Bernadette."

He leaned forward, placed his elbows on the table, and narrowed his gaze. "Hi, I'm Ned. When will you be ready to be married and have kids?"

The woman jerked back. She seemed shocked, but he bet she was just pretending. He hadn't met a female without an agenda this whole night. "Umm, I'm not sure. I want to be in love with the right person. Then marriage and kids can come later."

Hmm, good answer. Ned raised the stakes. "How long? A month? Two? You're already past thirty, and statistics show once your eggs reach thirty-five, your fertility starts declining, and chances of a healthy baby decrease by forty percent."

Was that a moan? He was only citing statistics straight from *Glamour* or *Self*. He forgot which one. Her lower lip trembled but he had her full attention. "I'm only twenty-nine," the woman whispered.

"Right on the precipice. I would rethink your plan if you want to birth at least two children. You do want children, right?"

Another small moan. "Yes, I've always dreamed of having children."

Finally. A woman who knew what she wanted. He relaxed. "Me, too. I think we have similar philosophies. It's been a tough night, but I'm glad we finally met. I think I'm supposed to wait till the end, but since this worked out so well, how about dinner Friday night?"

Ding.

This short encounter gives a direct glimpse into Ned's character without boring a reader by telling. Dump a character into a situation and watch him fumble around. His actions directly relate to the type of character you need to explore.

In longer fiction, a writer can linger a bit more on character descriptions, and season the characters. You have more time to build up and hint at conflict rather than knock the reader over the head with the conflict. You have space to simmer sexual tension and the banter between characters. Readers love tension in their books, so you need to have your characters unveil their secrets and demons at a slower, more leisurely pace.

With my book *Everywhere and Every Way*, one of the main conflicts is my heroine's inability to have children due to a hysterectomy. I don't reveal this fact to the reader until the midpoint of the novel, but there are hints sprinkled in for the reader and the hero to pick up on. When it is finally revealed, many of the readers' questions are answered and the pieces of the story slide together into an easy puzzle the reader enjoys solving. The heroine's drive to live a complete, joyful life shows up in her determination to enjoy her career and embrace the opportunities she does have. Readers know this about the character because they've seen her actions starting on page one, but they don't know why she is this way.

Here's one scene from the hero's POV, which helps the reader depict Morgan's—my heroine's—mind-set.

"So, you travel a lot."

She nodded. "Yes. My home base is wherever my client sends me."

"You have no need to settle down?"

"No. My career is at its peak, and I have no intention of sacrificing my opportunity at success."

He paused. Considered. "You're very ambitious."

She stiffened, and he got the feeling he'd misspoken. Her voice snapped back to the cool, formal tone he was used to. "Yes. And so are you. I happen to like my life the way it is, and I have no intention of changing it."

"Ouch. Didn't mean it as an insult. Just an observation."

Her shoulders relaxed slightly, but Caleb knew there was more to her reaction than he realized. There was a pain there, a bruise in her soul she didn't want to poke at. A vulnerability that called to him. He tamped down on the impulse to push a bit more, reminding himself there was no need to know the secrets of his temporary business partner. In six months, they'd never see each other again. Better to set up the rules now.

This example shows that career is a priority in Morgan's life, and she refuses to apologize for it, yet Cal senses a deeper, unspoken conflict. You can set a lot of emotion and intent in a few words or a sharply drawn scene, as in this quick snippet:

> "And you? What's your title in this crew?" she asked.
>
> "The grumpy one."
>
> Her giggle charmed him. Cal swam closer. The wet camisole outlined every flow and curve of her body, making him burn. He tried to concentrate on their conversation. "What about you? If you had to place a tag on yourself, what would it be?"
>
> It was a while before she answered. Her voice was a whisper of sound. "A fighter."

There are many ways to create a fully-developed character people can relate to. I fully believe our characters change as we age and grow as authors and in life experience. The characters we write about usually reflect something in our current stage of life. For instance, when I was eighteen years old, I desperately wanted to write adult romance, but my characters came out flat. I had no idea how a grown woman with a career acted. I had no experience with such a heroine, and I didn't know what type of conversations she'd have or what running a business was like. Sure, I learned tons from reading about these characters, and I could research, but I couldn't make myself feel something I hadn't experienced.

Does this mean you can't write about a situation or character completely different from your experience? Absolutely not. But be warned, it's a bigger stretch to write about, for example, a mother's love for her child when you have no relationship with a child and have never experienced any type of bond with a child. I avoided writing romances with single moms when I was in my early twenties, because I couldn't relate and I found it boring. But when my brother became a father, I was fascinated with my new niece. I became immersed in all kinds of baby stuff, like first words and the joy of seeing a child's love. After that, I was more interested in reading those stories, and I identified more with writing about that kind of connection.

I wrote *The Marriage Bargain* at a time in my life when I was in dating hell and began brainstorming ways to find a perfect man. I stumbled upon a love spell book to find your soul mate, which consisted of writing down the exact qualities you need in a man. Since my heroine was also desperate to save her family home and needed a large amount of money, I paired it with her search for love in a comic twist of humor. Take a look at my opening scene:

> She needed a man.
>
> Preferably one with $150,000 to spare.
>
> Alexandria Maria McKenzie stared into the small homemade campfire in the middle of her living room floor and wondered if she had officially lost her mind. The piece of paper in her hand held all the qualities she dreamed her soul mate would possess. Loyalty. Intelligence. Humor. A strong sense of family and a love for animals. A healthy income.
>
> Most of her ingredients were already cooking. One hair from a male family member—her brother was still pissed. A mix of scented herbs—probably to give him a tender side. And the small stick for ... well, she hoped that didn't mean what she feared.

Right away, you get a sense of the heroine and the lighthearted, humorous feel for the book. I used my own experience, combined with a lot of fiction, and was able to deliver a character readers still e-mail me about.

Sometimes it is simply a matter of age and experience that helps deepen and change our writing. I couldn't write an adult novel at the age of sixteen. But, as I grew older, my writing's raw, passionate edge rose to a more restrained, yet deeper level—I was a woman who'd experienced life.

Use the messy emotions in life to infuse characters with depth. Heartbreak is good. I remember looking back at some of my stories, and how I wrote excessively and dramatically about breakups and loss. I had a different view, and my characters reflected this. When someone broke my heart and tore it into tiny pieces, I crawled out of the experience battered and wary, but grown up. Reading my work afterward was a revelation. My hero and heroine matured. I wrote less about emotion and more about the nuances of emotion within the relationship. I could never have written like that before because my heart had been whole, untouched, and unbroken.

One stage is not better or worse. It just is. Everything I examined from the past thirty years has something special shimmering within it. Life changes, and one experience is replaced by another. What is lacking in one stage is fulfilled in another. It's our job as writers to examine and embrace each stage of our careers and how our writing has changed. This will directly affect the way we write characters.

We face many pitfalls in trying to create a solid character. For instance, I personally despise perfect characters. Humans aren't perfect, so characters can't be either. We are all messes, filled with issues from our past, our school days, and our heartbreaks. We have committed failures and grown insecurities. We make mistakes. We choose the wrong people to love. Our experiences influence our characters. And the richer the character, the more memorable they are to the reader. I want to identify with the people I'm reading about, balanced with a touch of fiction. Make your characters real but larger than life.

I don't want to read two pages of my heroine doing laundry for her son. I know she does laundry and has household chores, but I don't want to be reading in lieu of doing laundry, only to be reading about laundry. I want to read about the good parts, which is why I paid for your book. I want kissing and angst and sex and heartbreak and love ever after. If she needs to clean, you can tell me about it in a one-line narrative that merely sets the stage, and then get to the good stuff.

Give your characters quirks or weaknesses. Think hard about the stuff you do that annoys your spouse. I make a mess while cooking, so my husband comes in and cleans up behind me. That will give you a hint right away to our personalities: he's OCD and I'm a free spirit. I could care less about a sink full of dishes or peas on the floor (which the dogs will eat anyway). My husband *needs* the counters clean and the dishes done. These are real-life traits readers identify with. Take the basic stuff, twist it, make it more vivid, and you have a scene readers can laugh at and relate to.

Here's an example from *The Marriage Bargain*. This short exchange between my hero and heroine clearly shows their personality differences in the most basic of ways.

> Alexa squirmed in her seat as the silence in the black BMW stretched between them. Her husband-to-be seemed just as uncomfortable, and he chose to focus his energy into his MP3 player. She tried not to wince when he finally settled on Mozart. He actually enjoyed music without words. She almost shuddered again when she thought of sharing the same residence with him.

For. An. Entire. Year.

"Do you have any Black Eyed Peas?"

He looked puzzled by the question. "To eat?"

She held back a groan. "I'll even settle for some of the old classics. Sinatra, Bennett, Martin."

He remained silent.

"Eagles? Beatles? Just yell if any of these names sound familiar."

His shoulders stiffened. "I know who they are. Would you prefer Beethoven?"

"Forget it."

In *Searching for Someday*, my heroine had an issue with stuttering. In scenes where she was nervous, I showed her lapse into a stutter, as well as the techniques she used to stop herself. I didn't detail her past until later in the book, when the reader was ready to take a breath.

There is no limit to the freedom we have for our characters. From a hero with autism (Graeme Simsion's *The Rosie Project*) to a paraplegic hero (Jojo Moyes's *Me Before You*) to a protagonist who never speaks (Mia Sheridan's *Archer's Voice*), our writing is limited only by our own imagination.

Give me characters that struggle with addictions or demons from the past. Show them in the workplace, failing spectacularly.

With my novella *Searching for Disaster*, I opened up with my heroine engaging in a one-night stand. It was a pivotal, dynamic scene because it set the stage for a choice she'd have to make in the future, one that concerns this man she begins to care about and getting high. I wanted to ground the reader in a scene that would affect the rest of her life and the rest of the book. Don't be shy about detailing the ugliness in the world or the bad choices characters make. This is what makes them real. Here's an example of the moment her path turned toward disaster. My heroine, Izzy, just received a bag of cocaine in her dormitory room, and the man she'd slept with tells her to get rid of it.

"You don't have the right to tell me what to do."

His gaze burned. "Maybe not, but I'm asking. Something happened between us tonight. I'm not into magic and bullshit, but there's a connection

I feel with you I want to explore. I can't do that if the stuff in that bag is more important than me. Toss it, Izzy. I'm asking."

The tiny room tilted around her as shock hit. She had just met him, and he was asking her for a sacrifice. Wasn't it really just a way to control her? Shouldn't he be willing and able to accept her exactly the way she was? After all, she wasn't a druggie. She liked to take an occasional hit of coke. Why was that so wrong?

As she stared at him, the room filled with a rising tension and inner battle of wills. The bag behind her became a symbol of what path to choose. Yes, she'd never experienced such a physical encounter, one that seemed to raise sex to a higher level into the mental and emotional. But she refused to allow him to set rules. She could get rid of the bag if she wanted to. That wasn't a problem. The bag had no power over her.

But she didn't want to.

Izzy stepped back, as if to protect the item she'd sacrificed the unknown for. "No, Liam. I'm asking you to let it go. Just trust me—it isn't a big deal."

Slowly, the knowledge that she'd already chosen leaked into his eyes. He jerked away, a flash of pain carved in his face before it was quickly smoothed over by a distant expression. He nodded. Rose from the bed. And dressed.

"I'm not going down this road, Isabella," he said softly. "I'm not built for it, and I'm not about to watch what happens next." He paused, hand on the knob. "See ya."

He left.

Izzy stood still in the empty, silent room. Slowly, the bitter rage swept in from deep inside and caught her in its vicious grip. It might be the enemy but it was what she'd known and lived with her entire life. In a way, it was safe, so she embraced the violent emotions with zeal.

How dare he give her an ultimatum. He was like all the others. Judgmental. Arrogant. Only able to make decisions based on logic rather than accept the unknown chaos life demanded, and she was better than that.

Better than him.

Filled with righteous rage, she tore open the bag and grabbed the vial. The blindingly white powder beckoned and promised forgetfulness. Justice.

Silence.

Izzy unscrewed the vial.

Boring characters are boring people. Don't be afraid to make them different; don't be afraid to push them. In *Searching for Always*, **many readers**

commented on my hero and heroine's anger issues. It unsettled them at first, but as they progressed through the book, they discovered the reason for all that anger. Sure, I received a few bad reviews because my characters weren't happy-go-lucky, easy-going people. But who cares? Make your characters real. Make them interesting.

A likeable character can be just as riveting. Alexa, my heroine from *The Marriage Bargain*, is a pretty even, happy person. But she constantly worries about her weight and forces herself to eat salads. She wants to rescue the world, but her passion gets her into trouble. And she's fierce, so she's unflinchingly honest.

Maggie, my heroine in *The Marriage Trap*, is difficult. She's sexually experienced, a bit broken, sarcastic, and a real pain in the ass. She's not an easy character to love, but the payoff at the end of the story is bigger because of that. When she reveals a dark secret from her past, her behavior makes sense, allowing readers to become emotionally invested.

Give readers a payoff.

My favorite heroes are the ones that are so screwed up I can't believe I'm still reading the book. Yet, I grip the pages because they are so vivid that I need to see what happens to them. Linda Howard's hero in *Cry No More* was a hired killer and he terrified me. Christian Grey, from *Fifty Shades of Grey*, was an infuriating alpha control freak, but readers reacted to the chemistry between him and Anna, plus his hotness factor coupled with his hidden brokenness. Pepper Winters writes some deeply dark, disturbing heroes that make me so mad I want to throw my Kindle. But I always pick it back up. J.R. Ward is a master at character creation, and her Black Dagger Brotherhood series depicts a tight-knit group of vampire and shifter men who are alpha, problematic, frustrating, and hot. Readers devour this series due to its vivid characterization and raw appeal.

Even in a light, contemporary romance, heroes can make wrong choices and treat the heroine poorly. I can forgive that if I feel like I'm getting to know them and will eventually get my payoff. The payoff comes when the hero is brought to his knees and must redeem himself to the heroine. It's a secret contract between the reader and the writer that is sacred. Yes, I know the characters are screwing up terribly, and I kind of hate them, but I'm invested and believe in their growth.

write naked

Depicting a character at her breaking point is a powerful way to connect with the reader, but it must be done wholeheartedly—you must push this character to the limit of her strength. When I'm invested in a story, it should be a roller coaster of character growth, steadily bringing me to the black moment where a hero or heroine feels as if the world has splintered and everything will be lost. Here's an example in my book, *Searching for Beautiful*, where my hero suddenly comes face-to-face with his demons. The scene unveils from my heroine's point of view, allowing the reader to experience her emotions.

> "You need to get out." His jaw clenched, and he practically hissed out the words. The serpent seemed to be whispering the commands in his ears. "Now."
>
> She almost left. Knew it would be better. But she'd reached a turning point, and had one last shot at getting him to break. Open up to her. Give her a chance to let her love him. In this room, tonight, the demons needed to be sprung.
>
> "No."
>
> A growl rose from his throat. "Not fucking around, Gen. It's not safe here."
>
> "I don't want to be safe from you." She glanced pointedly at the boxing bag. "Nightmare?"
>
> The pain carved in his face made her want to weep; wail; leave. But she stayed, swearing to see it out to the ugly end, no matter what the result. They owed each other this much. "Yeah. I get them now and then, so I prefer to work it out of my system. Alone."
>
> "Maybe that's the problem. You've been alone too long."
>
> "Not up for this now. Go back to bed and we'll talk in the morning."
>
> "What if I don't want to talk?"
>
> He muttered a vicious curse. "Don't. I'm not safe right now."

The setup is the struggle for the truth. Once my hero confesses, my heroine must try to help him heal.

> "The days kept passing, and I got used to existing again. But when I looked at my wrists I remembered that night. So I started covering them up. Not seeing them. Pretending it didn't happen. Refusing to remember."

Every part of her body ached and burned to take him in her arms, cry, hold him. To finally know the truth, yet feel so distant from him ripped at her soul. He was slipping away from her, inch by inch, and in sheer desperation, she crossed the room and grasped his shoulders.

Those vacant eyes filled up with emotion. A wildness that made her dig her nails into his skin and shake him with the last ounce of her strength.

"But you did remember. It happened, and you survived. You're here now, with me."

"I'm not whole."

The simple words sliced like razors.

Don't be afraid to dive into emotions we all feel when we're struggling to deal with horrors in life or to form relationships of love.

Changing point of view is an important tool in revealing certain aspects of character to your reader. Using first person POV is a powerful technique to quickly bond a reader to a character. Emma Chase is a master at male POV, and her groundbreaking book *Tangled* introduces Drew Evans to the world. He's not the typical hero, but brash, arrogant, snarky, and perfectly imperfect. Here's a taste of his introduction:

Do you see that unshowered, unshaved heap on the couch? The guy in the dirty gray T-shirt and ripped sweatpants?

That's me, Drew Evans.

I'm not usually like this. I mean, that really isn't me.

In real life, I'm well-groomed, my chin is clean-shaven, and my black hair is slicked back at the sides in a way I've been told makes me look dangerous but professional. My suits are handmade. I wear shoes that cost more than your rent.

My apartment? Yeah, the one I'm in right now. The shades are drawn, and the furniture glows with a bluish hue from the television. The tables and floor are littered with beer bottles, pizza boxes, and empty ice cream tubs.

That's not my real apartment. The one I usually live in is spotless; I have a girl come by twice a week. And it has every modern convenience, every big-boy toy you can think of: surround sound, satellite speakers, and a big-screen plasma that would make a man fall on his knees and beg for more. The décor is modern—lots of black and stainless steel—and anyone who enters knows a man lives there.

So, like I said—what you're seeing right now isn't the real me. I have the flu.

Influenza.

This opening grounds us into his character. We know Drew's voice, manner, and can't wait to hear his story. What makes this setup even better is we discover he doesn't have the flu, but broke up with the woman he loves and is experiencing the fallout. Chase details it in a such a fresh way, we know this hero has never had his heart broken before.

Growth is the key to getting readers to fall for character, whether it's a duke, a shape-shifter, or a CEO. You may not get all of it in the first draft, but you're not supposed to. You'll gain a deeper understanding as you write the book, and that's when you go back to the beginning and *layer*.

Layering is crucial in character building. You cannot hit the reader over the head with obvious clues that scream, "My hero is strong," or "My hero is controlling." Use action, but don't throw all the ingredients from your cauldron at readers all at once. Reveal them in pieces, just as you discovered them as you wrote the book. Take readers there, and they'll buy every damn thing you write.

Many authors have trouble deciding how to introduce a character, and what details to include. I've learned the best way to open a book and begin a story is simple. Take your hero or heroine, and strip away everything they need and love. Snatch away every security blanket and drop them into the center of the action. See what they do and how they deal with problems. Start your story there, because readers can quickly identify with your characters when they're in a difficult situation.

Your heroine's car breaks down and she's broke and lost. Your hero has been working his whole life toward a promotion, and he tanks, losing his job and career. A misspoken quote hits social media and dethrones your heroine, thrusting her into the negative spotlight. Go big and set the immediate stage for disaster. Readers can relate to the feeling of everything safe being ripped away, and you will immediately create sympathy for your character.

Another way to create conflict and sketch out a character's personality is pitting opposite personality types against each other. In *Everywhere and Every Way*, my hero is a contractor. He's blue-collar, messy, wears ripped jeans and hard hats, and looks down at the white-collar workers who spend the day behind expensive desks in cushy, air-conditioned offices. My heroine is a home designer who wears only white. She's southern, polite, reserved, and neat. A simple conversation between the two erupts into banter that comes naturally from their different personalities. It was entertaining to write their relationship because they always surprised me. Here's a snippet of dialogue from their first meeting to set the stage:

"I'm in a bad mood, princess. Sure you want to take me on now?"

She tilted her head and regarded him thoughtfully. "Why don't you try me, Charming?"

His gaze narrowed. Oh, yeah, that got his attention. She tried not to get sucked into the depths of those amazing eyes, but she was fascinated at how quickly they could turn from smoke to cold steel. She wondered briefly what they'd look like when he was buried deep inside a woman. Whoa, what was that thought? Was she insane?

"What did you just call me?"

Morgan smiled at his slightly shocked tone. "Charming. If I'm playing the passive princess, you can play the part of the stud with brawn but no brains. Personally, I think the horses were the most interesting part of those stories."

In *Searching for Always*, my heroine and hero are complete opposites. He's a cop with anger-management issues. She's a yoga teacher who teaches the anger-management course. Watching the two of them banter was also a great way to increase the sexual tension, which is also important in a good romance novel.

Here's a scene from *Searching for Always*:

"I have a proposition," he drawled. "One kiss. Let's prove to each other we'd be a disaster together."

"I don't need a kiss to confirm you'd be a nightmare to deal with," she shot back. "You're an ex-smoker, workaholic, anger-ridden, meat eating cynic."

His fingers moved to caress her cheek, the line of her jaw, up to her temple. Little brushes of tenderness, contradicting the raw strength and power in those hands and body. Ready to crush her but choosing gentleness. The lust rolled over her in waves, and she fought back with all her power.

"And you're a tree-hugging, naïve, post-world hippie with a God complex," he retorted. "Vegetarian, to boot. Plus, a hardened criminal."

Arilyn growled under her breath and dug her nails into his shoulders with fierceness. "You know nothing about me, Officer! I am not naïve."

"My name is Stone, not Officer. Now shut up."

His mouth took hers.

Remember, flat, cardboard characters come from the fear of digging deep and getting messy. Use your own experiences to sketch real-life issues. Does this mean you have to create a dark, angst-ridden book with heroes that have horrific pasts and issues galore? No. If you don't want to write a book like that, then don't. If that's not your style, then don't write it. But you need the character background. Your hero or heroine's past is significant in sketching out their personalities, because we learn how to act from our past experiences. Or how not to act. Were you the shy one in school afraid of your own shadow, unseen for years, used to fading into the background? Were you bullied? Did your boyfriend cheat on you? Did your marriage fall apart? Did your father run away? Did you have an alcoholic or drug addict in the family? Did you lose a sibling? Did you have a sibling who surpassed you in every way? Were you ignored? Were you dirt poor? Did you have a hobby or passion that sustained you through the dark times?

Dig. Think. Play. Show.

As Anne Lamott said, "In general ... there's no point in writing hopeless novels. We all know we're going to die; what's important is the kind of men and women we are in the face of this."

No matter how much we work on understanding a character, it takes pages of writing before we become immersed in our character's entire being. Usually halfway through my book, my inner muse clicks to life and starts screaming like a banshee. "I understand! I understand!" I suddenly *get* my characters. I discover the secret piece of their soul that makes them unique, and from then on, the writing is so much easier for me.

Think about characters who are so real that multiple books have been written about them. J.R. Ward's brilliant group of men in the Black Dagger Brotherhood series. J.D. Robb's compelling Eve and Roarke. Janet Evanovich's adventurous Stephanie Plum.

What ties them together and makes them interesting enough to continue reading the books?

Character growth. A character arc. Somewhat damaged characters searching for something better. They are struggling with who they are, what they want, and where they are going. They don't have it figured out, and if they do, usually the author rips that away from them so they have to go back and start at the beginning.

That's the cycle of life, and it's what interests readers. When characters get the happily-ever-after, it's nice to know the hero and heroine are happily in love and strong together, but it doesn't end the story. If you've done your job as an author, you should be able to write a short story or another novel that continues their path. Love stories grow and change. Couples deal with difficulties. If you've given your characters their necessary arcs for growth, readers will watch them change within the pages of the book. They'll know that more changes will happen, but the characters will face them as a couple.

Romance guarantees a happily ever after, but there is also the happily ever after *for now*. No one believes that a marriage proposal makes everything perfect. But if you've set the stage, readers will be satisfied that your hero and heroine have reached a strong, solid place that will allow them to grow together. That's the hope of a happily-ever-after ending. That's also the satisfaction of watching characters struggle with their conflicts (individually and as a couple) to get to this place.

How do we go about creating extraordinary characters? Each author must find her own path, her own process. It's a process that also may change depending on the book she's writing.

After listening to dozens of best-selling authors, I've incorporated some great tricks for writing characters, but I have my own unique method I've learned to follow. I sketch out a basic background of each main character as a springboard. I create a physical description, name, basic past, personality traits, career, goals, and what makes him/her happy and what doesn't. Then I create the secondary characters and what I want them to accomplish. At this time, I also outline a very basic plot, one that's bare bones.

Then I start writing. I dive in, because I like the shock of submerging into my project without knowing everything. I enjoy discovering things about my characters along the way. I struggle in the beginning, usually rewriting the first three chapters multiple times. As I get further, I learn more about each character, and by the end, I can easily rewrite the book and fill in all the holes. I've figured out the inner workings of my hero and heroine.

I allow room in my book for surprises, such as secondary characters that walk into a scene and try to steal it. I remember when I was writing *The Marriage Mistake*, I created this hot guy in Vegas who was only supposed to be in a brief boardroom scene. Yet, he suddenly sprang to life and began flirting with my heroine. Taken aback, I followed the character, and chapters later, I realized he was not the main character and needed to take a backseat. I promised him I'd give him his book later. He agreed. That character was Sawyer, who became the main hero for *The Marriage Merger*.

These surprises, though, are unexpected riches. Which leads me to another important element in writing great characters.

Pay attention.

In her book, *The Artist's Way*, Julia Cameron says, "My grandmother knew what a painful life had taught her: success or failure, the truth of a life really has little to do with its quality. The quality of life is in proportion, always, to the capacity for delight. The capacity for delight is the gift of paying attention."

Pay attention both inside and outside the book. Inspiration may strike, or a scene may take a turn you didn't count on. These are your opportunities to let your characters breathe. You may need to follow the path, even if it goes into a dark woods or the scary, fairy-tale forest full of wolves and death. You still may have to go.

When you are writing a book, you are living in dual worlds. When I go out and see real people other than my family, my characters stay with me. I could be drinking and laughing with an acquaintance, but the slightest tug of my attention could send me spiraling into my fictional world, snatching a fleeting detail or revelation that is crucial to my story. I hold onto the thread with enthusiasm, pulling the frayed edge through the tiny holes in my mind. It is awe-inspiring and terrifying, because it's out of my control. It's the muse. All I know—and accept—is that my book is always with me, ready to spring forth at a moment's notice if I pay attention.

And that is pure delight.

································*Exercise*································

Use your work-in-progress to really think about your characters. Is there something you can do to help understand them better? Take a few minutes to try this exercise. Write down what your hero is most afraid of in his life, then sketch out a short scene where he is confronted with his innermost fear. How does he handle it? Follow the threads and see if you learned even one thing about your character that can help you in the book. Do the same thing with your heroine and then compare.

20

secondary characters that pop

"When writing a novel a writer should create living people; people not characters. A character is a caricature."

—ERNEST HEMINGWAY, *DEATH IN THE AFTERNOON*

If you are writing a series, secondary characters are critical to its success.

That's a big statement, but I'm going to try and back it up.

Secondary characters have always been important in books. Authors use these characters to broaden the seams of the story and add depth with layers of conflict, drama, or humor. Think of the hero or heroine's best friend, siblings, parents, co-workers, etc. Sometimes secondary characters have their own storyline as part of the book, and other times they are only in the story to help make the main characters shine.

Series have become extremely popular, and secondary characters are now in the spotlight. Readers enjoy trying to spot the next potential hero or heroine, and imagine him or her as the protagonist in the author's next book. If you properly set up the ending to your first book, you can get a reader to hit the preorder button for the next book, based on the power of your secondary characters.

That's good stuff.

I know I try to determine the next leading man or lady in a series all the time. When I was gorging on Nalini Singh's Psy Changeling series (which is up to book seventeen at the moment), I became obsessed with trying to figure out which secondary character would be next. I couldn't press the buy button fast enough. She also had me wait a long time for one of my favorite couples, but I was determined to read each book in order and get there in a natural way.

You must be skillful in sketching out your supporting characters. They must be interesting, but not so interesting that they overshadow the main storyline. As I mentioned previously, Sawyer Wells, a secondary character in my novel *The Marriage Mistake*, became a bit too big for his britches. Suddenly, I was writing him into *every* scene, until I remembered whose book it was. I quickly backed up, deleted some of his starring roles, and when he threw a tantrum, I promised him his own book.

He agreed and stepped back gracefully.

The same thing happened with *The Marriage Bargain* and Alexa's best friend, Maggie. When I wrote the book, everyone told me Maggie was more interesting than Alexa. Horrified, I realized she had a big, dramatic personality that overshadowed my heroine. I quickly rewrote her into a supporting role, and let her loose in *The Marriage Trap*, where she could be the star.

Secondary characters that pop are a gift. If they stand out, that's your indication they need their own story. But even characters you never think of as leading men or women can surprise you. In Christina Lauren's The Wild Seasons series, a secondary character called Not Joe became so popular, the authors decided to write an exclusive story featuring him entitled, "A Not-Joe Not-So-Short Shorts," which was only available in the book *Wicked Sexy Liar* at Target. Readers hunted down the book in order to snag this special short, showing how secondary characters can boost a series and also create amazing marketing power.

In *Searching for Perfect*, I wrote about a nerdy aerospace engineer whose older brother, Connor, taught him all the wrong things about women. I wrote Connor as comic relief. He was awful, and chauvinistic. Con-

write naked

nor was the antihero of any romance book. Even my editor sighed when she read the book, and told me Connor would never have his own story. That was okay, because I had no intention to continue his tale.

Until my readers began e-mailing me in droves, asking for Connor's story.

I was stunned. Why would they want to read about him? I made him unappealing! He had no story to tell! I went along, writing my other books, until I realized Connor had dug into my brain and offered me a challenge. Could I transform this antihero into a romance hero? Was it even possible?

I took the challenge and wrote his story, *Searching for Mine*.

It was one of the most satisfying books I've ever written, because I had to reach deep to find all the good stuff, and it challenged me as a writer. It ended up being an emotional story that readers really loved.

Write your secondary characters with care. Give them depth. Make them interesting. You never know when they will surprise you with their own book.

What are some solid ways of writing extraordinary secondary characters?

Give them a secret. Give them a big personality.

In my Searching For series, which features twins, I made Isabella the bad girl. She wreaked havoc on characters, and my readers weren't too sympathetic. But they still begged for her story, because she was intriguing. When I finally wrote *Searching for Disaster*, I challenged myself by taking Isabella out of the depths of drug addiction and into the starring role of her own love story. Don't be afraid to get into the muck with real characters. Get messy and offer something real to your readers.

Perfection simply doesn't exist. And if you are writing a perfect secondary character, make sure you surprise the reader with what lurks beneath that perfect surface. The junk is what makes a secondary character—really, all characters—interesting, and inspires the reader to try to figure out what can come next.

You want readers to buy the next book.

Humor is another way to incorporate interesting secondary characters. Secondary characters are perfect for lightening up tense situations and causing amusement in readers. In *Searching for Perfect*, Connor had caused a problem with the hero and heroine because he believed he was protecting his brother. He finally seeks out the heroine to make it right, but I needed to reveal his soft heart via his personality. I decided to use humor. Here's an example:

> Connor muttered something under his breath. "Nate loves you. He's trying to get over you, but it's like he's haunted all the time. Unhappy. He goes through the motions. Meets me and the guys for drinks, but he's like a shadow of himself. I think I was wrong."
>
> Her heart pounded so hard so loudly she swore his brother heard it. "About what?"
>
> "About you. I think you got scared, like you said, and freaked out. I think I judged you because you remind me of all these women who have hurt me, starting with my mom. But I don't want to do that anymore. Who am I to judge you? We all make mistakes. I'm a walking mess, but Nate's putting me through school now and I want more. Don't you?"
>
> "Yes," she whispered.
>
> "Good. You need to go see him. Get him back."
>
> "I'll need to prove he can trust me. You think he'll forgive me?"
>
> "Yeah. But you gotta come up with something good. Something epic."
>
> The hope let loose and sprouted. She had another chance. "I have to think."
>
> "Maybe you go see him in a raincoat, and you take it off, and you're naked underneath. Then you say I'll do anything to get you back."
>
> She rolled her eyes. "Dude, are you serious? That's so lame and over-done. Next idea."
>
> Connor glared. "Would've worked with me," he muttered. "I know! We deliver a big cake to his lab, and you jump out in a sequined bikini while the song 'I Apologize' is on in the background and beg his forgiveness."
>
> "Never gonna happen. Can you come up with an option where I wear actual clothing? It needs to be an emotionally epic moment, not physical."
>
> "I think you're going in the wrong direction here."

Invoking sympathy is another great tool for readers to bond with secondary characters. In Susan Elizabeth Phillips' book *Breathing Room*, Tracy is the hero's ex-wife who moves in with him in Italy. The situation is precarious, and most readers won't take kindly to embracing the hero's ex in a romance novel, but Phillips makes it work brilliantly by evoking sympathy. Tracy is pregnant and struggling to save her marriage. She's desperately in love with her husband who doesn't want the baby. Here's a sample:

> *Who are you?* she wanted to ask. *Where is the sweet, tender man I fell in love with?*
> … "You shouldn't have come here," she said when they were gone.
> He finally looked at her, but his eyes were as cold as a stranger's. "You didn't leave me any choice."
> This was the man she'd shared her life with, the man she'd believed would always love her. They used to stay in bed all weekend, talking and making love. She remembered the joy they'd shared when Jeremy and the girls were born. She remembered the family outings, the holidays, the laughter, the quiet times. Then she'd gotten pregnant with Connor, and things had begun to change. But even though Harry hadn't wanted more children, he'd still fallen in love with their youngest son the moment he'd slipped from her body. At first she'd been certain he'd fall in love with this one, too. Now she knew different.

Immediately, I am transfixed with Tracy's problem and am rooting for her. This was a daring way to create a secondary couple, but it works to strengthen the entire story arc.

Series are a huge part of the market now, so you need to carefully seed your plots. When creating the first book, make sure you sketch out who will appear in your follow-ups. Yes, there are always surprises, but you should know there will be either three, four, or more characters *planned* in the series. Give the reader a hint of what's to come, tease them with ideas of the hero or heroine's match, and firmly keep all your secrets in your back pocket until they shine in their own book.

With my Billionaire Builders series, I sketched out three estranged brothers, planning to give them each their own book. I also planted a lot in the first book, paving the way for their individual stories, while leaving room for surprises along the way. For instance, after the death of their father, the brothers are brought together to run the family business—a customized building company. Each of them experienced betrayal at the hand of another, and now they need to face the past and try to heal in order to save the company. I incorporate the sibling conflict with the mystery surrounding their mother's death, which is not fully solved until the final book. This keeps pulling the reader forward to discover the secret.

I also created a secondary character who had a previous relationship with one of the brothers. I hint at their conflicted past, but when her daughter is written into the story, I realized my final book will reveal the real father. Once again, this pulls readers into the next book in the series.

Surprises lurk at every turn, though. My surprise came when a young, sassy female walked into book two, and I realized she'd eventually need her own story. This would bring the series to at least four books. I hadn't planned for that, but I left room for the unexpected. The novella will be released this year, and hopefully bump up sales for the final book.

Be willing to write more books if your muse is calling. If the readers aren't buying, you can always return to the series another time, but hold onto your deleted scenes and ideas for safekeeping. You never know when interest in your series might be renewed—remember, every book becomes part of your backlist. That is the great thing about digital books: They have unending shelf life.

Your secondary characters are your trail of bread crumbs leading to the sale and must be treated with care.

Make them big. Make them unforgettable. Make them real.

Make them pop.

································ *Exercise* ································

Go over your body of work and write down all the secondary characters you've used for a new book. Write down the ones who haven't received their own story. Figure out why certain characters are more interesting than the others. By discovering the type of characters you are compelled to write, you are able to consciously bring these traits into future secondary characters in your work.

··

21

let's talk about sex

"*Literature is all, or mostly, about sex.*"

—ANTHONY BURGESS

There's never been a sex scene I haven't liked.

To write, that is. I've read some terrible sex scenes, but *damn* I'm good at writing them. I knew this at a very young age, too. Maybe it was the years of reading romance, or figuring out the types of characters I liked and letting the sex scenes naturally happen. I never shied at words, giggled, or felt embarrassed. I was proud when I nailed one (pun intended). I'd give my mother my pages, and the poor woman would try to skip over scenes too uncomfortably hot for her.

She'd ask me very nicely if I could write less sex in my books, and maybe have them not curse as much. I took it under consideration, then told her no.

She's never asked me again, but she still skips the sex scenes.

Now, sex means different things to different people. Sex can encompass foreplay. Foreplay can encompass a make-out session, heavy touching with clothes on, heavy touching with clothes off, and even reaching orgasm without penetration. I know many will disagree with me and retain their own opinion, and that is fine. I'm not here to talk technical issues, but I do want to talk about what sex encompasses in a romance novel and how extremely important it is.

That said, I hope I haven't lost all the inspirational or sweet romance writers out there: Please hear me out.

Sex, to me, is a deep, meaningful connection between two people on a physical plane. However, sex also occurs in the mind—this may be more accurate for females than males. I've read that the brain is the largest sexual organ. I agree. So, let's say, for purposes of this chapter, sex is both mental and physical.

You need sex to connect your hero and heroine in a romance. I don't care if it's open- or closed-door sex scenes, or no sex scenes. There must be some type of touch or kiss, otherwise you're not writing a romance novel.

Let's go over some of the genre categories and how sex scenes should be handled.

SWEET ROMANCE

The first book I ever read from Jayne Ann Krentz was actually under her pen name, Stephanie James, for Silhouette romance. I remember the hero and heroine never had sex, and a kiss was the furthest they ever went in the book.

Hell, I didn't miss the sex. The kissing was *that* good.

That's because Krentz is a master at the art of sexual tension—the buildup of banter and character play that sizzles on the page. When the characters finally touched, it felt like an explosion, though it was limited to one very hot kiss.

Any type of physical contact can feel like sex, if it's written correctly, exploiting all the hero and heroine's chemistry. That's one of the main reasons readers love romance. The relationship is primary at all times—whether it's paranormal, historical, or mainstream women's fiction. And this romantic relationship must have some type of sexual connection or the reader will lose interest.

Let's take Jojo Moyes's popular *Me Before You*. It's a brilliant story. But there's no sex. The most we get is an amazing scene with Will and Louisa at a party, and their perfect, soul-stirring kiss that makes the entire book worth ... everything. The relationship is carefully constructed, lengthening the sexual tension and emotion, until the kiss lets loose a torrent of sighs and tears.

Yeah, baby. Now, that's good sex.

Kristan Higgins writes powerful, emotional romance with closed-door sex scenes. Check out this tantalizing peek from *Anything for You*:

> "You're so beautiful," he said, and then he sat on the bed and tugged her down with him. He held her hands over her head, and kissed her for a long, long time, tasting her, learning her mouth. Then he let her hands go, smiling as they buried into his hair. Bit by bit, he undressed the rest of her, taking his time, tracing every bit of skin he saw, tasting it.
>
> "You're killing me here," she whispered, her breath ragged, and he lifted his head and smiled, and after a second, she smiled back. It wrapped around his heart, that smile, hot and tugging. "Hurry up, Connor O'Rourke."
>
> This was one of those moments of honest-to-God perfection, and he wasn't going to rush through it. No.
>
> He took his time instead.
>
> There was no complaints.

Connection is the glue in all sex scenes, no matter what type.

SEXY AND EROTIC ROMANCE

I love all types of romance, but I tend to write an open-door sex scene. Now, I've read books where the hero and heroine jump into bed, and the actual scene is pretty well constructed. It's well written, and technically accurate. The physical portion is fine. But my heart? My libido?

Nope. I'm feeling ... nothing.

Why?

It lacked connection, emotion—something that bound me to the characters and transcended me into the physical aspect of their relationship. Sex always needs to be wrapped in some type of emotion for romance readers. I don't care if it's a one-night stand or a temporary hookup. I still want emotion or the scene will leave me flat.

In *Searching for Beautiful*, the sex scenes are more erotic, but I make sure to use emotion and connection to set the scene. In this example, my hero, Wolfe, and my heroine, Gen, are best friends fighting an attraction.

Gen has been rejected on a date and is feeling vulnerable. Wolfe busts in to check on her, and all that simmering tension finally explodes.

"Look at me."

The rough growl was full of danger, command, heat. She was helpless to disobey, leaving the safety of the window to turn and face him full-on. He reached out and tipped her chin up.

Blistering, raw lust shot from his eyes. As if they were glowing from under the sea in the Caribbean, she tumbled into the depths of a gaze that promised everything with a Warning: Danger label attached. His grip tightened, refusing to allow her to retreat, and he crowded her space by taking another step between her thighs. The sill dug into her lower back. His scent drowned out everything but the need to touch him, feast, taste—the delicious mix of lemon and soap and cotton surrounding her.

"I need you to listen closely, because I'm only going to say it once. Understood?"

Her lips parted. This was no friend. This was a deadly man with an agenda. Transfixed, she nodded, unable to form words, mere prey beneath the command of a dangerous predator.

"I'm done with excuses and conversation and politeness. I'm over this bullshit of your questioning the power you have to grip me in a vise so tight I can't even breathe without wanting you with my last breath. I'm tired of walking around with a dick that won't go down when I catch your scent, or look at your sweet curves, or imagine being buried deep within you. Are you still listening to me, Gen?"

"Yes."

"Good. Because tonight I'm going to fuck you. All night. If I was a true friend, I'd walk out that door and give you the space to rebuild your walls. You deserve that. But I'm a selfish prick who needs you in my bed so bad I'll trade my soul to the devil for one taste of you. Still listening?"

"Y-y-yes."

"I'll give you three seconds to run. It's the smart thing to do. Just walk away from me and we'll never mention this again. We'll go back to being friends, push this whole episode aside, and go on pretending. But if you're still standing here after that, you're mine. Every part of you. And I promise you'll never question your ability to cast a sexual spell on a man so deep and encompassing he'll spend the rest of his life comparing you to every other woman he touches."

write naked

Erotic romances are structured so each sex scene is critical to the story. If you deleted the sex scenes, the story would not hold up. That's the contract you have with your reader when it's branded as an erotic romance. Never leave a woman unsatisfied, because this genre is heavily focused on the power of a woman's pleasure.

Erotic romances many times include hardcore, porn-like, dirty sex. Some fabulous erotic writers have this mastered to a fine art, unafraid and unapologetic in using crude language to strip down sex to an animal-type hunger. For example, dirty-talking heroes are one of my favorite weaknesses. There's just something so intense about a man who tells you every wicked, dirty thing he wants to do. In detail.

Darker Elements of Erotic Romance

BDSM is an acronym for Bondage, Dominance, Sadomasochism. BDSM was famously introduced to the world in *Fifty Shades of Grey*, though erotic writers have been penning BDSM romances for years. The sex scenes with BDSM can be milder, as a way to introduce the reader, or they can dive into full depth for a more intense experience.

What many readers find so addicting with BDSM romance is the intensity of the experiences, and the mind games played between the submissive and the dominant. That power play is critical in commanding readers' attention, even after the actual sex scene is over.

The foundation of BDSM is full consent, where the submissive truly holds the power. There is usually a contract in play about the terms beforehand. Another intriguing element for readers is the level of communication between the hero and heroine. Sexual play is detailed and discussed ahead of time, which gives readers a comfortable level of tension without fear that the hero or heroine will go too far.

Some popular, bestselling BDSM authors with large followings include Cherise Sinclair, Lexi Blake, Stacey Kennedy, Joey W. Hill, Sierra Cartwright, Shayla Black, C.D. Reiss, and Maya Banks.

Dark romance is another popular form in which all rules are broken. Dark romances put heroines in fearful situations, and use sex as a connection to the fear. Many contain elements of nonsexual sex, kidnapping the heroine, criminal heroes, and various erotic punishments.

These authors deliberately include darker aspects within the story for a specific reason, and readers are usually warned on all outlets what the story contains. Readers who enjoy a dark romance cite the excitement of not knowing what's going to happen, with no safe rules applied. The erotic elements are usually much edgier in dark romance.

Once again, in both BDSM and dark romance, emotion and connection between the hero and heroine is key in creating a successful story.

SEXUAL TENSION

Sex is a primary part of a romantic relationship. Touch is critical to a hero and heroine, and we should be comfortable with all aspects—from the brush of a fingertip to the passionate kiss to the slam against the wall, take-me-now intensity of sex.

But the sexual tension leading up to the act is just as important—maybe even more so. The buildup toward a physical scene should be dragged out with delicious precision and give the reader enough to tease, but not yet satisfy. My favorite way of doing this is through banter, which is usually disguised as fighting, but it's so much deeper than that. Banter is the edge of dislike, frustration, or the attempt to deny what the character really, really wants. Tell me I can't have something and I want it bad. Heroes love that type of challenge. Women like to fight attraction if it doesn't work out well in their head. They are stuck with more analysis, which can be interweaved within the sexual attraction. Using these aspects is a writer's greatest weapon in writing sex.

Remember the old series *Moonlighting*? Viewers watched each week to see if Maddie and David would finally hook up. While they dragged this on—tortuously—every week, the show delivered satisfaction through banter and connection between characters. Their verbal foreplay was legendary. Other examples of this are the now defunct shows *Castle* and *Bones*. Half the fun was tuning in regularly to see when the characters would finally stop fighting and just kiss.

Here's an example of ramping up sexual tension with verbal banter in *Searching for Always*:

And just like that, the annoyance was back. "I don't need this type of complication in my life right now," she snapped. "You're a client. We can't blur the lines."

Those lush lips that had bestowed such pleasure now treated her to his famous sneer. "Don't give me that crap. As I just said, I'm not your client, and you're not my real therapist. You counsel me to control my temper, which is getting frayed right now by your sad excuses."

She bristled in fury. "Excuses? I don't need an excuse! We kissed, it was good, I'm over it. Let's move on. The last thing I need is a pushy cop wrecking my life."

He got in her face. "Lady, you wrote the book on pushy. A relationship with you would be a nightmare. But you can't deny we'd steam up the sheets together."

She gave up poetry for this? He was rude, crude, and owned no soft edges. First he kissed her, then he yelled. Even if she wanted a transitional lover, he was all wrong. Arilyn refused to back down, even if she had to tilt her head back to eyeball him. "Classy. You can go ahead and steam them up with someone else."

He shook his head as if disgusted by the thought. "Can't. Chemistry this good is rare. It may piss me off, but we have to explore it."

She gasped. "In your dreams! It was a complete fluke. I'm not exploring anything with you!"

He studied her with hard eyes, and the man did something so outrageous she didn't see it coming.

He kissed her again. Just manhandled her, pulling her in and planting his lips over hers for a long, deep, thorough kiss that curled her toes and revved her body right up to Ferrari status.

Sexual tension can be used in an entire book, half the book, or even just to heighten a single scene. But if our brain is the biggest sexual organ, we writers must include the tension within our sex scenes.

WRITING A GREAT SEX SCENE

Writing sex is about steeping ourselves in the glories of being stripped down to our animal-like tendencies. It's carnal and raw. It's powerful. Sex is an act of supreme faith, removing clothes and standing vulnerable before another human being, asking to be loved. Asking to be wanted. Asking for acceptance.

If you are trying to write a sex scene by moving body parts around on the page, you will fail. You must strip your characters down to their essence, reveal their vulnerabilities, and take the leap with them. You must remember the first time you bared yourself to another person. You must steep yourself in the scents and sounds of lovemaking: from the tangle of damp sheets, to the sheen of sweat on the skin, to the musky, tangy scent of arousal hanging heavy in the air. Sex is messy, and it rips our civility and barriers away. Let your reader be immersed in the experience, because this is the place where raw, naked emotion occurs, and she should not miss the best parts.

As I said, I love all sex. I read voraciously in every type of genre and appreciate each one for what it is. This also helps me bring some freshness to my own writing.

My advice? If you tend toward sweeter romance, try reading a romance with a graphic sex scene. It's good to see how the author handles the interaction, both physical and mental. If you tend toward erotic type scenes, pick up a sweeter story and examine the way the characters experience sex in a more innocent manner. Analyze the tension and the buildup, and judge whether the kiss brings satisfaction to the reader.

Writers are commonly advised to read in other genres, and I firmly believe they should read other categories in romance, especially for the sex scenes.

With the explosion of *Fifty Shades of Grey*, women readers flocked to romance books afterward because they connected with the relationship, the romance, *and* the sex. It was such a wonderful boon for romance authors everywhere, because readers tried different types of books, and romance authors were given the opportunity to build their readership. Countless readers have told me they rediscovered their love of reading since *Fifty Shades of Grey*, and, to me, that is the best thing a reader can ever say.

That *Fifty Shades of Grey* explosion reminds us not to judge anything until we try it. And we should urge ourselves to step out of the cocoon of books we prefer and try those outside of our comfort zone.

READER EXPECTATIONS

Be careful what you promise your reader, because one big mistake can break a reader's trust. If your cover and blurb screams sweet romance, she will not be amused to find dirty words and graphic sex scenes included. Same with the promise of an erotic romance—readers won't be happy with only one mild sex scene.

Your cover, title, blurb, and category make a promise. Remember to keep it. Label your book erotic, sexy, or sweet, if possible, just so you can help your readers find what they are looking for.

Sex scenes need to be included to further the story, not just because you don't know what else to do with the characters at that point. I can't tell you how many times I've been stuck and tried to throw my characters in bed together. Fortunately, my muse is a bitch and my characters so stubborn, they fight me when I try to make them do stuff they're not ready for.

Sex scenes in all forms, whether sweet, sexy, or erotic, are a crucial part of the romance genre. By infusing emotion and connection into each intimate scene, your reader will be left with a big smile on her face.

Exercise

A hero and heroine are locked in a room together. They are strangers, but wildly attracted to each other. They will be together for twenty-four hours before anyone rescues them. Now, write a sex scene. If you are an erotic author, write a kiss sequence with no intercourse. If you are a sweet romance author, write a dirty, kinky sex scene. This scene is for you only—no need to judge yourself or share. But it's important to see how you'd handle intimacy in a different manner, as a way of strengthening your writing skills.

22

theme

"*To produce a mighty book, you must choose a mighty theme.*"

—HERMAN MELVILLE

At the beginning of my writing career, I couldn't tackle theme. It was too hazy of a concept for me to understand. I was still focused on solidifying my grasp of building sexual tension, creating witty banter, and dealing with the all-important character arc. Theme was something I never thought or honestly cared about.

As with most careers, the more I grew and studied craft, the more I began to realize how important theme was to a book, *and* a series. The first time I ever tried to understand theme, it was at an RWA conference. I was lost and ultimately left the session early.

The second time I was enthralled. My pen danced over my paper, trying to catch every last precious drop of information because the almighty lightbulb had switched on. I finally *got it*.

Theme is the overall truth of your book or series. When you figure out the theme you want to write, it resonates throughout the book, working behind the scenes while the reader follows the story. In my opinion, when when the reader closes the book that has a theme, a deep satisfaction lingers much longer than a book with no theme.

Theme pulls the loose threads together and makes your story whole. The hardest part is teaching you how to do it.

I'll start with some examples. In my Marriage to a Billionaire series, I hadn't yet figured out how to incorporate theme. I wrote the series without understanding what I was doing. I knew this: My goal in the four-book series was to explore the power of family. I wrote about an Italian family, the Contes, and each book detailed a specific character. The story always returned to the matriarch of the family, Mama Conte, a wise, older woman who taught my characters the lesson of the book.

As I wrote each book, I found myself including details of what family meant to each character and each character's struggle to define who they are and understand their romantic relationships.

This was not something I consciously included, and I never waved my hands in front of the reader, smugly showing off my skill as a writer. At the time, I only knew that these details made my book richer and created a perfect link to the next story. In turn, they created a beautiful arc. At the end, I felt satisfied, as if I had done my job well for readers.

My next series was the Searching For series, a spin-off of the Marriage to a Billionaire series. I wanted to check in on my original characters while still creating a fresh, new series. I already tackled the themes of a marriage of convenience and family. My new topics became the dating world and the power of friendship. My original heroine, Alexa, had two younger twin sisters in *The Marriage Bargain*. I decided to peek into the future, writing about her sisters, in addition to a secondary character my readers had fallen madly in love with in *The Marriage Merger*—a young, scarred teen named Wolfe.

This new series gave me the ability to introduce readers to a whole new world, while retaining characters that I knew they loved. With this series, I made a conscious effort to develop theme. Friendship was at the core of each book, with each book in turn tied to a circle of best friends who created a matchmaking agency.

I have been lucky in my life to be blessed with many close friends from junior high. These people know me—and they know my defenses and weaknesses. They also love me unconditionally, because they *chose* to love me as a friend—they are not forced to love me like a blood relation.

Exploring that world, and the dynamics of close female friendship, was the key to the theme within the series.

This past year, I penned the final book in the series, *Searching for Disaster*. I ended up writing 45,000 words in ten days because my muse was flooded with emotion and wouldn't shut up. I didn't sleep or eat, I just wrote furiously for hours, pouring out this final story, knowing all the loose ends needed to be tied together in order for my theme to ring true.

When I reached the end, I cried for an hour straight and went to bed.

Friendship took center stage, but again, I wasn't consistently hitting my theme over the heads of my readers. Theme is subtle, like a wisp of smoke in the air, blanketing the book in a deep, satisfying comfort. Within scenes and dialogue, I carefully and quietly seeded the theme so that readers never knew I was there.

At key points throughout the book, I created scenes showing how friendship was the foundation, in this way bringing the reader back to the main theme of the book.

Here's an example from *Searching for Beautiful*:

"I hate love," Arilyn said grumpily. Another shared look between Kate and Kennedy.

Gen sighed and drained her drink. "Me, too. Love sucks."

Kennedy raised her hand in the air and flagged down a waitress. "That my darlings, is why they created alcohol. Another round, please."

They looked at each other and began to laugh.

Here's a snippet from *Searching for Someday*:

"I say we don't need any men. I say screw them."

Kate nodded at Kennedy's booming statement. Funny, her head was floating a bit off the top of her shoulders, but she looked good that way. Almost like a fairy. "Yeah, you're right. We don't need men at all. All we need is each other."

"And good movies," Arilyn chimed in.

"And wine," Ken declared. "Forever and ever!"

"Girl power!" they all shouted.

She didn't remember what happened afterward. The room drifted, warm and cozy, and her friends voices were like music to her ears.

write naked

In each book, the heroines are strong because they have each other to lean on. With the ups and downs of their romantic relationships, I bring the characters back to the power of friendship, my main theme of the series.

Don't forget to use secondary characters to reflect your theme—either human or canine. In *Searching for Someday*, I introduce a disabled pit bull named Robert, who earns the respect, friendship, and love of my hero. In *Searching for Always*, I wrote about an abused Chihuahua named Pinky. Her road to recovery is cushioned by the love from my hero and heroine, but it's Robert who helped her truly heal. Pinky was terribly afraid of Robert and it took a while for her to build trust. Slowly, the dogs form a bond, and the theme of friendship between canines resonates for my precious secondary characters. Here's a peek:

> "Stone." His name shot out in the room like a cannon ball. He turned to Arilyn, worried, and saw her staring at something behind the counter. Her face reflected a bit of shock mixed with something close to joy. "Come over here. Slowly."
>
> He took a few steps toward her and followed her gaze.
>
> Pinky was sprawled out on Robert's back, her small head resting on his, nestled in the soft spot between his ears. Her eyes were half-closed in ecstasy. Robert didn't move, his chin comfortably resting on the ground, a look of pleasure planted on his face, a half doggy grin widening his mouth.
>
> And in that moment, something broke inside Stone's chest.
>
> A gooey mess of junk poured out, making his eyes sting and a tightness squeeze his heart. Damned if that wasn't a sight to see. The two survivors, together, happy and safe.

In my newest series, the Billionaire Builders, based on HGTV, my theme is forgiveness. The dynamics center around three estranged brothers who are forced to work in the family business together. Their family holds many secrets, and a pain no one wants to remember. I forced these characters to confront not only their respective heroines, but each other, moving them toward forgiveness. That theme beats within the little moments of my scenes, a rope guiding the reader forward.

Not only do they eventually need to forgive their father for his cruelty and their mother for her abandonment, but they must also forgive each other for the individual pain each suffered.

Here's a snippet from *Everywhere and Every Way*, showing the brothers in a bar, working toward forgiveness.

> How strange, after all these years of refusing to talk about the incident, that it was finally revealed in a dingy bar on the anniversary of his mother's death. The wound that had festered for years broke open, and oozed clean. The truth rang out in his brother's voice. For the first time, Cal accepted the reality and realized though he'd screwed up, Dalton had never set out to seduce his fiancée. It was almost as if he could feel his mother's presence wrapping around them, desperately trying to get them to listen to one another.
>
> "I'm sorry, Cal. I really am."
>
> The apology struck home. Emotion clogged his throat, so he just nodded. His voice came out gruff. "Apology accepted."
>
> And then they sat awhile longer, not talking.

Think about what is important to you and what you want readers to remember about your book. What are your characters really fighting for? What do you want to explore? What will connect your series to give readers a deeper, more meaningful experience beyond the regular happily-ever-after.

STORY THEMES

I think there's another type of theme to be explored. I call it *story themes*. This is different from the overall theme you are working on in a specific book or series. The story theme runs on a deeper level, identifying what type of story you like to write. It's a theme that's present in your *collective* works.

When a writer looks over her body of work, there are always certain phrases, characters, or ideas she returns to. Think about that word you just love to repeat, that your editor always points out. Or how you tend to write blonde heroes, virgin heroines, secret baby stories, or marriages of convenience. We *all* have our favorite stories that we like to tackle, but a story theme is bigger.

Let's take my books, for example. It didn't occur to me I was exploring the same story theme throughout my books, because each of them was a unique experience. But when I dug further, I realized I always had one theme that linked all my books.

I am too broken to deserve love.

Yep. That's the one that seems to be my Holy Grail of story theme. I'm fascinated entirely with the concept of love, and how difficult it is for so many people to accept they are worthy. That is the main theme I explore within various story formats. Whether it's my hero, heroine, or even a secondary character, readers will stumble across my endless analysis that never fails to fascinate me: *Am I ever really whole enough to love and be loved?*

Think about the books you write. Explore and analyze the core of your story. Do you like to investigate how your characters can overcome their past? Do you like to analyze how one mistake can change a future? Are you fascinated by how one major heartbreak can ruin a hero or heroine's belief in love?

There are endless story themes, but I bet each of you have your own personal favorite, one that's repeated in each of your stories.

As *New York Times* best-selling author, Kresley Cole advises, "Develop your book's theme: As a reader, I crave certain themes. If a writer provides what I'm craving, then I'll be back for more. Emotion + Theme + Sorcery = potential bestseller out of the gate."

Embrace your story theme to understand who you are as a writer and what you want to explore. Embrace your book's theme to deepen your writing and satisfy more readers. By using both tools, you will take your writing to a new level.

·······························*Exercise*·······························

Examine your body of work and determine your story theme. Then analyze your current book to see if you have developed a theme, or if you are lacking one. Finish whatever draft you're working on and then go back and edit with an eye toward layering the theme of the book. Think about who you are as a writer and what you truly like to explore. The answers to those questions will help you build the backbone of your books.

··

23

the sagging middle

"Middles challenge us to find our tenacity and our patience, to remind ourselves that it is within this struggle—often just at the height of hopelessness, frustration, and despair—that we find the most hidden and valuable gifts of the process. Just as in life."

—DANI SHAPIRO, *STILL WRITING*

What is the hardest part of a book for you to write? That's one of the most consistent questions I get in interviews. And I think it's important every writer knows their limitations and what they need to work on. We have our own unique strengths and weaknesses. I have several weaknesses I'm always trying to improve, but the two constants I struggle with are setting and middles.

Especially middles.

I now understand why writers call it "the sagging middle." I started a story strong, with all the intentions to finish with a flourish, when suddenly it deflates like a limp balloon. I feel as if I've reached the blank, boring space that I can't seem to fill with anything but crap.

Now, the sagging middle probably exists for me personally because I don't plot or outline in major detail. As an organic writer (I'm a pantser),

I like to figure out things as I go. I may know the beginning and end, but I usually sketch the middle with hopeless optimism and a smug smile that says to my muse, "No worries. I'll know what happens when I get there."

I never know. Ever.

My only consolation is all the other times I've struggled yet managed to flesh out the middle. And they're numerous. The seams of a story will either hold up or collapse under the weight of the middle. This is the part of the book in which we truly discover who our characters are—and that's why once we've been through the middle we usually need to go back and edit the beginning.

For me, this is also the most exciting time, because toward the latter half of my middle, I suddenly *get it*. A big lightbulb goes off in my head, revealing why I was writing this story in the first place. The characters finally show me who they are. But to get there, I need to be open to discovery. I need to show up with only one guarantee: I will be completely miserable for the next few weeks while I work on the middle. But it will be worth it.

Doesn't the hardest stuff usually deliver the biggest payoff? The beginning and end are amateur hour. Anyone can do that. But to slog through the middle of the story, to show up and be consistent, to handle the unglamorous nuts and bolts of a story, that's where the true writing champion shows up. This is what gives me the most pride.

I stuck around to write my middle. I didn't give up.

All of your writing practice leads to this point. For me, this is where I may need to pause to research a bit. When I was writing *Any Time and Any Place*, halfway through the book, I discover my hero is passionate about stargazing. And that he has a telescope. This discovery was unexpected. I was just writing, and suddenly I had this intense knowledge that he loved astronomy. Now, this fit with the overreaching theme of my book—finding one's own home in life—but that knowledge came to me later.

As I'm writing this scene, slogging through the mud pit of word carnage, I realize I *despise* astronomy. I flunked it in college. I like looking at the stars but couldn't tell you where the Big Dipper is.

I was cranky. I bitched about having to stop writing the book and spend a few hours online researching constellations, stories about Greek mythology, and what type of damn telescope he'd have.

Research seems like a big time suck, but we usually discover things that make sense much later. I needed that time to think about my hero, why he loved stargazing, and how it connected to my heroine. And when I figured out that my heroine also loved the stars, I rewrote a fabulous scene in the book, and threaded it through the middle, all the way to a grand gesture that tied up the ending.

See, the middle is time to take a breath and air out your story. It's okay to spend some time figuring them out, even if you're a plotter and know exactly what's going to happen. The middle is where the surprises are hidden—not the coveted beginning or end. It's a wonderful secret buried in the muck, and only the writers who take the time and energy to harvest the story will find it.

This is where trust comes in. You must trust your previous writing experience to find your way. Trust in your muse and your characters. Trust that you will be shown the way, but that it may not be the road you originally intended.

I'm not saying the middle will be fun for you to write, but I've learned, at least, to trust. That takes away a lot of the sting.

And if you're one of those writers who adores writing the middle of the book, good for you.

For the rest of us, remember great rewards come from hard work. You may discover realizations about your character by digging into the heart of the story. Great realizations come by creating habits. Those are when the lightbulb moments come crashing over us. But you have to show up to get it, and you have to write the middle.

················· *Exercise* ·················

Take a few hours while writing the middle of your book and research something for your characters. It can be the hero or heroine's career, a hobby, or even a location they might visit. Breathe some air into the story, and allow yourself to look at it in a fresh perspective. Research is tricky because it can drag us in and keep us from writing, but I also believe it's crucial to writing a great book. Even if your research material doesn't make it into the book, you will know more about your characters and story—and that will translate to the page.

24

emotion

"I think being able to capture emotion so perfectly that your reader feels everything you [the writer] felt while writing the story plays such a huge key to success. If you can make the reader's heart race and breath catch, making them feel as though they're falling in love right along with the characters ... or if you can make them grieve and mourn the loss of another, as if the character was someone they knew, then your story will be hard to forget, and just might spread like wildfire."

—MOLLY MCADAMS, *NEW YORK TIMES* BEST-SELLING AUTHOR

Our lives are extraordinary.

Most of us just don't know it.

Writing women's fiction and romance celebrates the extraordinary moments that make up our lives. And the best moments are full of emotion.

The joy of a mom looking at her beloved child's face. The first curl of passion and hope when lips first meet. The raw and aching grief of losing a family member. The shattering pain of a broken heart when you're left by someone you love. The giggles from your best friend as you drink cocktails and talk about boys. The shaking, petrifying fear of illness. The stunning beauty of the ocean, mountain, or the large, twisted oak tree in your backyard.

Each is simple, yet these are what make up the fabric—the essence—of who we are and the lives we live. This is what we must tap into to make our stories roar to life. Use your experiences and create brushstrokes on the page; channel every type of emotion in your scenes and the words will suddenly pulse with a heartbeat.

If you are not brave enough to face it all, your story's potential will never reach full bloom.

How do you make sure your book has this type of emotion?

I've found emotion is a consistent element in romance, and most authors cite emotion as the key element of a book's success—and their entire career. Unfortunately, I've found emotion to be one of those tricky elements that books either have or don't, and it's a bit hard to teach. Sort of like voice.

But let's try, shall we?

When I'm learning something, I go directly to the masters—the keepers on my bookshelves. We all have those dog-eared, worn paperbacks that you don't lend out tucked away in a secret file. For some, those shelves are now in digital format, but you can still scroll through your Kindle and pick out the books you'd happily read all over again.

Take one of those books, and go directly to a scene that stands out in your memory. Reread it, analyzing why this scene intrigues you. Pick apart the emotions the author packed this scene with and how they affect you.

How is the scene structured to deliver an emotional punch that hooks a reader and makes her crave more?

Is it the vulnerability? The truthfulness of the interaction? Is it the explosion of built-up tension?

Whether it's a declaration of love, a confession of a secret, or a strong alpha male showing a softer side, there is something in that scene that you can relate to—an elusive element the author gathered up and showed on the page.

write naked

Now, examine how the scene makes you feel. Does it touch you? Anger you? Frustrate you? Turn you on?

Do this exercise with a number of your favorite books, and you will begin to see a pattern. Each person identifies with unique emotions. We seek out books that take those emotions and deliver them in a solid, one-two punch, by first setting up the dynamics of the scene, then driving it home to the reader. And then we try to find more books that do the same.

I've noticed many things about my writing and reading habits by doing this exercise. First, I've always been a sucker for a damaged, proud, alpha male who struggles throughout the book before finally reaching a breaking point. That moment is a key emotional scene that I consistently seek in other books and write in my own books. Simply put, it just ... gets me. Every damn time. The vulnerability of truth hitting a man while he faces the one woman who won't let him hide anymore.

In Susan Elizabeth Phillips novel *Kiss an Angel*, the prideful, arrogant, mighty Alex Markov is literally brought to his knees when he saves the life of a tiger and shows the heroine he really does love her. It's such a stirring scene; every time I reread it I tear up. It's full of emotion. Here's a peek at how the scene unfolds (spoiler alert!):

> "So what?" Sheba sneered. "This isn't about Daisy. It's about you. What's it going to be, Alex? Your pride or the tiger? Are you going to lay it all out for love, or are you going to hold on to everything that's important to you?"
>
> There was a long silence. Tears had begun to stream down Daisy's face, and she knew she had to get away. She pulled back from Brady, then froze as she heard his angry sputter.
>
> "That son of a bitch."
>
> She whirled back and saw Alex still standing in front of Sheba with his head high. But his knees were beginning to bend. Those mighty Romanov knees. Those proud Markov knees. Slowly, he sank down into the sawdust, but at the same time, she knew she had never seen him look more arrogant, more unyielding.
>
> "Beg me," Sheba whispered.
>
> "No!" The word was ripped from Daisy's chest. She wouldn't let Sheba do this to him, not even for Sinjun! What good would it do to save one magnificent tiger if she destroyed the other? She ran through the back door and into

the arena, kicking up sawdust as she flew toward Alex. When she got there, she caught him by the arm and tried to drag him to his feet.

"Get up, Alex! Don't do this! Don't let her do this to you."

He didn't take his eyes off Sheba Quest. They burned. "It's like you once said, Daisy. Nobody else can demean me. I can only demean myself."

He turned his face upward, and his mouth tightened with scorn. Although he was on his knees, he had never looked more glorious. He was every inch the czar. The king of the center ring. "I'm begging you, Sheba," he said flatly. "Don't let anything happen to that tiger."

Daisy's hand convulsed around his arm, and she dropped to her knees beside him.

Another way to create emotion on the page is to develop heroes or heroines who screw up big time, make me mad, and then have to fix it. This is human, after all—to err. And watching the characters eventually emerge with a renewed understanding and forgiveness is beautiful to experience. Here's a peek at *Searching for Always* (spoiler alert!). My hero has broken up with the heroine, given up his rescue dog, and needs to make things right. I use emotion but stay true to my character, who will never be the mushy hearts-and-flowers type.

Stone Petty stood in the waiting room. There were two other clients there, staring at him curiously. In full uniform, looking badass and sexy as hell, he held Pinky.

Clad in her pink sweater and bling collar, the dog looked as if she had found nirvana. The look of complete love and trust filled her eyes and her body, and emanated in waves of endless energy.

Pinky had forgiven him.

Her fingers flew to her mouth and pressed against her lips. "Wh-What are you doing?" she asked.

"I got her back." Those inky eyes were fierce, seething with raw emotion in a twist of lust, need, and determination. His muscles seemed locked and loaded, as if ready to explode in a rush and take her with him for the ride. The heat in her belly uncurled and spread through her veins like wildfire until she could only tremble, helpless under his gaze and the promise she so wanted to believe in.

"I fucked up. I won't again."

The room was eerily silent. "How ... how do I know?"

"You don't. Look, I'm not a poet, and I suck at these big endings and declarations like in a sappy romance novel, but I love you. I love you, body and mind and soul, and I love this rat fink dog more than I can ever say in just words. So I'll show you every damn day instead. I want to be in this with you. I know we're gonna fight, and you'll piss me off, and I'll piss you off, but I think we were meant to be together from the moment I first laid eyes on you and decided I didn't like you."

Another favorite way of mine to evoke emotion is the lightbulb moment. This occurs when a character realizes she doesn't have to take the blame for something pivotal. Again, I can relate to the feelings of guilt, the sickness of not believing I'm enough, or the frustration of not being able to change the past. All of these basic conflicts and character developments in romance novels revolve around emotion.

This is done brilliantly in Kristan Higgins's *The Best Man*. There's a scene where the hero, Levi, tells the heroine the truth about the car crash that killed her mother. He has discovered details that can help her deal with an issue that's affected her entire life. In this way, he gives her a priceless gift, and afterward their relationship deepens to a whole new level. The power of the exchange is so delicately balanced, and brutally deep. Higgins is a master at depicting emotion.

In *Searching for Disaster*, my heroine needs to come to terms with her past drug addiction and allow herself to be loved. There's a powerful scene between her and her father, who is a recovering alcoholic. The exchange allows my heroine to see her life in a whole new way. Here's a peek:

"I'm afraid," she whispered. "Afraid I'm not good enough for him. Afraid I'll hurt him. Afraid I'll be weak one day and use again and destroy everything."

"I'm afraid, too. But trying to protect people by being afraid is wrong and against everything they're trying to teach us. We're addicts, Izzy. But we're people, too. We screw up and cause pain, but we also fight through the bad stuff. We love fiercely and try hard and do everything we can to be the best of what we are. God forgives you. We forgive you. You told me you forgive yourself, but if that were really true, you'd let Liam love you."

Once you get an idea of your emotional triggers—and the strong scenes that depict them—you'll be in a better position to know when you fail to deliver them in your writing. Go back and reread your pages to see what fell flat. It's most likely an avoidance of triggers, or trying to finish, rather than lingering on the emotional qualities of the characters within the scene. Dive deeper. If you're worried about being overdramatic, don't. This is not the time to hold back. You can polish and tweak in later drafts, but writing the messy, honest, disturbing stuff in your characters is the key to the treasure.

A reader may have a hard time explaining why a book falls flat, but it's probably a lack of emotion. Your writing can be perfect, your plot flawless, your setting stunning, but if there's no emotion on the page, if you can't make the reader *feel* something, they won't care very much about your story. And then no one will buy your book.

························*Exercise*························

Journal time. Pick an emotional memory and write it down. Don't pause to think too much, structure, or edit. Write it down exactly as it happened and everything you felt. It doesn't matter if your prose isn't pretty, you can use concrete words like mad, sad, cry—anything that keeps the pen or keyboard moving. When you've finished, read it aloud and note what made that moment stand out, and how it ties into emotion. The more comfortable you are exploring your own emotional triggers, the easier it will be to write those moments into your book.

write naked

you don't have to love all your children equally

"Literature is strewn with the wreckage of those who have minded beyond reason the opinion of others."

—VIRGINIA WOOLF, *A ROOM OF ONE'S OWN*

This chapter may get ugly.

We're going to discuss hard truths about preferring some manuscripts over others. We're going to admit we have our "favorite" children.

I do.

I've heard many writers repeat the same statement over and over when asked about their favorite book they've written:

I could never answer that question. I love all my children equally!

or

My favorite book is always the one I'm working on now.

That's nice, but I'm telling my own truth here, and the above two statements are *not* true.

First off, usually my least favorite book is the one I'm currently working on, because 80 percent of the time I hate its guts.

Second, labor is forgiven, but never forgotten. I don't forget those books I bled out for, lying panting and wrecked with spasms of failure. And some of that writing became my greatest work, but I still don't like it as much as other books.

The exception here is my youngest son, who, though not a book, put me through awful labor, as previously described. But there really is a difference between flesh and blood—I harbor not an ounce of resentment regarding the way he came into my world.

Back to the books.

Some are a gift. They are actually fun to write, and even when you're struggling, you still seem to glow with a positive attitude, knowing you'll eventually get where you need to be. *The Marriage Bargain* was one of those books. *The Marriage Merger* was another. I was never lost. I may have slogged through some iffy parts, but I was mostly pretty happy and fulfilled.

Searching for Someday was a book I really hated. It was the setup of not only a new series, but a spin-off from the Marriage to a Billionaire series, so I had high expectations. I remember quite clearly coming out of my office in tears and yelling at my husband:

"This book is going to tank my career!" I paced back and forth. "It's horrible. I should title it *Searching for a Plot!*"

"It can't be that bad," my husband said. He always says that. I always get mad because it seems he's not really *listening* to me. He can't fix this!

"It is, it is," I cried. "Nothing is happening. And I keep writing about this dog Robert who's paraplegic and—"

"What do you mean he's paraplegic?" my husband asked. "How does he walk?"

"He has a scooter, or drags himself around on his belly in the house."

He stared at me in horror. "That's horrible! Why did you write about something like that?"

"I was inspired by the real story!" I yelled back. "I want to write about something real, and there's a parallel between the hero and heroine, but right now there's nothing but scenes with the dog."

He tries to help. "Maybe your editor will like it."

"She'll hate it! She'll fire me. Should I make them have sex? Maybe if I forced them to have sex the book will get better?"

"Will your editor like that?"

"I don't know! I tried to get them to have sex before but they didn't want to, so maybe I'll just try and make them."

He blinks. "Babe, you're the writer. You can make them do anything."

"You don't understand! Forget it—forget this whole discussion. Just be ready to put the house up for sale 'cause this is it for me. I swear I'm not joking around!"

End of conversation.

I'm proud of *Searching for Someday*, but it's still not my favorite, and it never will be. I wrote it under a large amount of stress, and I felt strained through most of the book. I worked hard on that thing, and I don't like to think about it.

When I was struggling with one of my other books, I remember talking to my friend Amy, trying to explain that I just didn't love it. I loved the concept and the characters, and thought it was quite brilliantly put together, but I didn't enjoying writing it. And I couldn't figure out why.

Her words have always stayed with me. She said, "I think we need to give up on the idea of loving every single book we write. Sometimes our skill can take over, and even if we're not enjoying the process, or experiencing excitement over the story, that doesn't make the book bad. We're too attached to our feelings of *how* a book is going. I think we need to let go a bit and just accept that some books we love more than others, and that is totally okay."

Yeah. It was. By secretly admitting to myself that I didn't enjoy writing the book, I was still able to experience great satisfaction and happiness with the finished product. It was like lifting a burden from my soul. I was going through some life changes at the time, and there were a lot of distractions happening in my work. I realized all those years of my perfecting craft, writing book after book, had helped in a critical way. My muse was able to sit back and coast. It was a great book, because I had studied my craft and created it on a more unconscious level, rather than planning every thread. Though I felt as if the writing was flat, whenever

I went back a few days later to reread a passage, I was impressed with the quality and emotion.

I did my job successfully, even though I didn't feel completely present.

And I believe I had earned that right. I was a professional, and this wasn't my first rodeo. There are some wonderful assets that come with having experience and writing steadily for over twenty-five years.

The follow-up, *Searching for Beautiful*, poured out of me. It holds a piece of my past and a piece of my soul; it's deeply personal. I cherish this book more than any other for many reasons, and I always smile when I see the cover or hear someone mention it.

My indie projects also bring me a level of joy, because I get to play and experiment with these books. I love stretching my creativity, diving into first person, new adult, erotic BDSM, or paranormal. Experimenting helps me offer a fresh perspective, clears my palette, and allows me to feel like I hold the final determination of whether it was successful or not.

Remember the first time you hit a best-seller list? I bet that book was one of your favorites. If you haven't hit one yet, when you do, you'll fall in love with that book. You'll never forget the experience of a phone call letting you know you are now a best-selling author.

Each book is an experience in our life and represents the entire body of work.

Bottom line? Each book I've written is imprinted on me in various ways, and I've embraced the concept. You should, too. That's what makes each book unique, because a different piece of you is in each one.

················*Exercise*················

Take a few moments and compose a list of your body of work. This can contain short stories, poems, books, essays, or even journal entries. Decide which pieces of work you love, and which ones you don't. List the reasons why. It's good to see if you can trace an event in your life to the reason for your struggles with that particular book, or identify emotions with the ones you love. It's also a way to go over your writing journey and pause to reflect where you have been.

················

26

the hard stuff

---

*"All writers are vain, selfish, and lazy, and at the very
bottom of their motives lies a mystery. Writing a book
is a long, exhausting struggle, like a long bout of some
painful illness. One would never undertake such a
thing if one were not driven by some demon whom one
can neither resist nor understand."*

—GEORGE ORWELL

Finally. The chapter I get to unburden all my crap and revel in the
knowledge that some of you—hell, almost all of you—truly get it. I attend
writing conferences for all sorts of reasons. Besides making a connection
with other authors and my readers, attending them gives me time away
from my office to take a breath and immerse myself in new insights. When
I return from these conferences, I'm usually exhausted. My voice is a tiny
squeak of sound, my liver is screaming for detox, and I'm craving to crawl
back into my safe house and not see people for a long, long time. But it's
all worth it for one reason.

I get to bitch nonstop over cocktails with my author friends.

And they don't give me any puzzled looks, sighs, or stares with
suffering patience across the table from me. I can talk about imaginary

people for hours, and no one looks bored. With sheer delight, I babble nonstop about the mechanics of sex scenes without worry. I am finally with my people!

So, besides not wearing real clothes, having intense conversations with my dog, hearing voices nonstop, and feeling like my head will explode from all the Technicolor, riotous ideas flooding my brain like a mad sugar rush, these are the things that plague me in the writing world.

'*Writing is the only thing that, when I do it, I don't feel I should be doing something else.*"

—GLORIA STEINEM

WRITER'S GUILT

I have writer's guilt. All the time. It's that feeling that I should be writing. Let me break down the days of when I carry guilt, and when I don't.

No guilt: This occurs on days when I write a minimum of four thousand words of a *new* manuscript. After, I have the entire evening to spend with my family, doing mom stuff, eating a relaxing dinner, and kicking back with a book or my favorite show, because I had a great work day.

Guilt: Every other day.

I can't win. This career haunts me, it always has. When I'm not writing, I feel guilty. Like a pebble caught in a shoe, or an irritating bug bite that flares up, the thought arises in the middle of great fun and times of relaxation: *You should be writing.*

I kinda hate it. I wish the voice would go away. Sometimes I just don't want to write, or I'm having a hard time writing and I want some peace so I can get back to it with a better attitude.

But the voice doesn't go away, so I try to decide what I can truly live with and what I can't in a regular workday. Writing two thousand words a day is a solid, average performance. It's acceptable. Yet, if I quit, I feel as if I should do more. Could do more. Maybe just another five hundred words? Am I being lazy?

write naked

Forget it if I only crank out one thousand words or less. I become a loser in my mind. When my husband comes home and asks how my day went, I groan and complain that I didn't write enough new words and maybe this career isn't going like we originally planned. Maybe I won't get another contract since I'm not producing. Maybe ...

He usually tunes out by then.

When I'm cranking out work at high speed, there is usually some sort of deadline involved, and I ignore my family, slip into a state of panicked, raw creativity, and do little else but write. I rarely shower until my husband forces me. I walk around in a fugue state, eating "healthy" meals like peanut butter slathered on a Hershey's bar, and consuming megacups of coffee in the morning, while switching to wine at 5:00 P.M. on the dot. I am not pleasant to be around. I don't even like myself. I feel mother's guilt, wife's guilt, and I'm-a-terrible-person guilt. But the work gets done, and I swear to you, it's all worth it.

If I write a good book, there is no sacrifice I won't make to get there.

Well, except legally giving away my children. Or my dogs. Or my husband. (Umm, no, sometimes I'd like to give away my husband.) Anything else goes.

My days could be filled with an editing project, social media, or promotion. I could have a twelve-hour workday, but at the end, if I'm short on new words, I feel guilty.

In what type of career should this guilt be acceptable? Rationally, I refuse to give into such weak emotions. Logically, I think this type of *bleeding-for-your-art-all-the-time* sucks.

In a yogic way, I realized it doesn't matter what I think. It's what I *feel*, and I can rationally accept it, decide to not write for whatever reason, and continue my day. I can accept it, even if I'm not okay with it. But when I write and the words are good ... those are the best days of my life. I sleep so much better. I relax. I feel happy.

And then the next day comes, and the cycle begins again. I make do and find calmness where I can.

True peace comes only in one place.

Disney World.

Mickey Mouse demands full attention, along with the children. Disney also kicks your ass. You end up walking several 5Ks, and when your exhausted body finally falls into bed, the voices are too tired to bother you. Ah, the punishing glory of Disney is a place of peace for me. I return home mentally refreshed, ready to go back to work because I've been away from my computer. (Checking social media while waiting in ridiculously long lines doesn't count.) It's pretty impossible to feel guilty for not working while at Disney. A win-win for me.

SOLITUDE

A few weeks ago, I texted my husband a grocery list and asked him to stop at the store after work. Being a wonderful husband, he agreed, but when he arrived home, there was no protein powder for my smoothie shakes.

(Just an aside: I have a diet based on my writing schedule and the seasons. In warmer months, and when I'm not on deadline, I eat vegetarian, organic food, and remember to at least walk or stretch. When it's winter, or I'm on deadline, I should be arrested by the food police. This, however, was a healthy transitional time.)

So, I let him have it for not buying the protein powder. I worried what I was going to do the next day, as my meals were meticulously planned out. He said, "Why don't you go to the store after the boys go to school and get it yourself?"

I blinked. Was he a madman? "You want me to go out?" I asked.

"Umm, yeah. It's good for you to go out sometimes."

I backed up like he was a monster. "I can't go out! I wish I could put barbed wire around the fence so no one thinks they have the right to ring my doorbell, trudge around my property looking for the meter, or save me with the Bible. I don't like people. And I don't want to go out."

Frustration spiked from his body. "But you're always the hit of the party when we go out!" he said. "Everyone wants to sit next to you, and drink with you, and you say all the time how much you love them."

"I'm lying. At the time, I do love them, but I'd be happy to stay forever in my beautiful office with my imaginary characters and have no one bother me."

"Babe, I think you need psychological help. If you want the powder, you have to go out for it."

I stomped away, promptly clicked on Amazon, ordered the powder on speedy one-day delivery, and got my revenge.

The point of my story is this: No other career relies on being alone as much as being a writer does. Writing is done alone. You can pretend you have the safety net of your friends, editor, agent, or family. You do not. Because in writing, there is no safety net available. You're in the abyss, alone, with a blank page. You can drag your laptop to a crowded café, but make sure you realize there is no one with you on your journey except the characters you create. And sometimes, they can be a real bitch to deal with.

The better the writing goes, the more time you usually spend alone. There have been many times where I've forced myself to stop writing because I had to get the kids from school. Once, I drove past the school because I was still in the fog of my book. Another time, I parked outside the school but never went in to get them, because I was staring out my window, listening to music, thinking about my book. When people try to say hello to me, I feel weird. My voice is scratchy, unused. I'm kind of afraid. I just want to go back home.

Look, I did not pick this profession for the conferences, parties, and networking at the bar. I picked it because being alone and creating books are a part of me. I need the quiet to blossom. This is normal for writers.

Now, when I force myself to leave my comfort zone, I always do well. I've forced myself to schedule more public speaking events, and I love hanging out with fellow writers. I've made long-lasting friendships and connections I love dearly. But the transition is hard, and I know I've spoken to many authors who agree. Usually by the third day of a big conference, I see that look on everyone's face—like they're half here, half back in their office. They don't want to socialize or talk. They want to get back to work, because that is the only place writers feel whole.

DEADLINES

If you want to be a career author, or have any hope of regularly publishing, you need deadlines. Constant deadlines. Traditional or self-published, it doesn't matter. Print usually demands a longer delivery schedule. Digital is a bit tighter. But if you don't work on deadlines, it's too easy to keep tweaking the book, distracting yourself with "business" stuff, or even deciding to delay the release to do something you think is better.

But, honestly? I hate deadlines. They tire me. I know if I can just write on a normal, even schedule and do a manageable amount each day, I'd meet my deadline with no problem.

I thrive on adrenaline. I seem to work better when I've wasted all the time imaginable to deliver the book. Then I go into crisis mode. I complain nonstop, refuse to cook (not that I do that anyway), work insane hours, forgo sleep, and promise God if he will just allow me to deliver this one book on time I will never, ever, ever do this again.

Do you know how unsexy it is to write an erotic scene with unwashed hair, hairy legs, mismatched pajamas, a robe dripping in chocolate stains, and a deer-in-the-headlights look on your face when anyone dares to even peek their head into your office? Ugh. Even my husband doesn't want to be around me when a deadline is lurking. Actually, he's the one that eventually shows up and threatens to make me sleep in the garage if I don't shower.

I run into real crises during my deadline period. I delivered my book, *The Marriage Mistake*, to my editor at Simon & Schuster, which was about to go to publication in a few months. They called it a crash publication, which basically meant they'd pulled out all the stops to get this book in stores, with no lead time.

My editor called me and told me the book had serious problems. She gave me a choice: I could rewrite the entire book within seven days or I could decide to have the book published months later.

I'm not a quitter. I told her I'd do whatever it took to get this book back to her in seven days. I promised I would eat, sleep, and hole up in my office in order to deliver it *on time*. And then I remembered something important.

I have children.

Two children. Little children. Children who needed me to take care of them. Forget the two dogs, my husband, and all the other stuff going on in my life. So, I quietly told her that I had two kids and wasn't sure if it was possible to do in seven days.

The following was our conversation.

EDITOR: *Pause.* "Well, you'll just have to give your children away for the week."

ME: "Umm, give away my kids? Who would take them?"

EDITOR: "Someone has to take them! You can do this. I know you can! Just make some arrangements."

ME: "*Okay.* Yeah. Sure, I'll do it! I'll give away the kids, and write night and day, and we will publish this book on time!"

EDITOR: "That's the spirit! I knew you were a rock star! Call me if you need anything."

I hung up the phone and trudged into my office to speak with my husband, head beginning to spin with sheer panic.

HUSBAND: "Hey, honey, how was your talk with the editor?"

ME: "She didn't like the book. I have to rewrite it. In … well … in seven days."

HUSBAND: *Blinking.* "Isn't that hard to do?"

ME: "Yes." *Pause.* "So we have to give the children away for a little while."

I won't bore you with further details on that conversation. Let's just say the children remained safely at home. At some point, they were clothed, fed, changed, and maybe even played with. I finished the book. My husband didn't divorce me. So technically I'd call it a happily-ever-after editing story.

······························*Exercise*······························

Write down every rotten, stinkin', crappy thing that writers have to deal with. Hook up with a writing buddy via e-mail. Exchange complaints, validate each other, and have a cyber cocktail. Then get back to work.

··

27

perfect endings

'And will I tell you that these three lived happily ever after? I will not, for no one ever does. But there was happiness. And they did live."

—TRUMAN CAPOTE

I've written twenty-nine books, and this is my thirtieth. That doesn't include the six manuscripts I wrote before the first was published. Almost every single time I reach the end of one of my books, I cry.

One time I finished a manuscript and felt nothing. I struggled with this story more than others, and numbness overtook me. I took it as a sign the book sucked, which was how I felt the entire time I wrote it. I closed the document, disgusted with my failure, and myself. At the time, I decided it was the end of my career.

Two weeks later, I read the book from beginning to end without stopping because it had to go to my editor—and I bawled like a madwoman. After letting it settle, and walking away, I realized this: It was a really good book. I just needed to take some time to step away from a project that had taken over my life. I needed to see it as a reader, not a writer who'd memorized every single word.

Writers handle the ending of a book in different ways. Crying at the end is a sign for me that the book is good. It is also a release of all the raw emotion, struggle, and grief that this journey required of me. I'm joyous. I'm sad. I'm wrecked. I'm depressed. I feel like I'm experiencing PMS and pregnant hormones to the one hundredth degree.

In the writing of a book, I have lived and breathed life into characters. We (the characters and I) have lived in a bubble together. They are my children, so I've loved them with passion and disliked them on occasion. They made me cry and questioned my abilities as a parent. But in the end, seeing them grow up happily-ever-after and leave me is completely heartbreaking.

When a book ends, it no longer belongs to you. It belongs to the world. It's a gift from you to the world, and it's precious, but the world may not like your gift. They may post terrible reviews and insult you on Facebook and Twitter. They may laugh at your creation. But none of this matters. My advice to you is to toughen up, move on, and deal with harsh comments—because you must understand that your work is public and not everyone will appreciate it. You shouldn't whine, or defend yourself or your work. You should lift your chin and remain a stoic. Some reviewers actually want you to *thank* them for their cruelty, because they say it's for your own good. Like a Hollywood celebrity acting in a film, once you release your book, it is to be judged, mocked, and analyzed.

It no longer belongs to you.

Some will love it. Oh, they will love it like their own, and hold the book to their chest, stroke the pages, tell their friends, or take the time to leave you a lovely review. *This* is worth everything.

We must try to focus on the good. We write for many reasons, and one of them is to give joy, happiness, and escape to our beloved readers. Imagining so many treasuring your words will help you release your precious child to the world. Declaring a book finished is a time of dizzying pride, satisfaction, and freedom.

But how do you know when it's really the right time to end your book?

How do you know you've given the reader everything necessary: satisfying scenes, strong emotions, interesting dialogue, a solid plot, and enough conflict to keep the pages turning?

Ah, my young Jedi, you will just know ...

Nah, I'm kidding. Sort of. Every writer completes his story differently. I write linearly—from page one, all the way to the end. I rarely skip around or write scenes out of order, unless I am experiencing crippling sewage and need to trick my muse. Other writers have no problem writing the scenes that intrigue them, then jumping around with neon sticky notes and graphs and charts.

You've reached the end when your story has a satisfying, happy-for-the-moment conclusion. Or not. You've reached the end when your characters have grown, and you know the heroine on the last page is different from the heroine on page one. If there's no change your readers can see or feel, then you haven't come to a satisfying conclusion, and the book is not yet done.

The ending to your book is different from the ending to your plot. Plot can be pieced together, then carefully pulled apart to see if it holds up. A cold read helps me determine if I've messed up the time line or if there are gaping holes that don't make sense. A cold read is when you have enough time to step away from the book for a minimum of a week (preferably more), then go back to read it straight through. When I go back, I usually end up adding a crucial scene that's missing, deleting excess information, and smoothing and polishing anything that feels rough. But a true, satisfying ending is a completely emotional experience in romance fiction. It's not the conclusion to your plot. No writer should be satisfied when her critics say that the plot was solid. Yeah, that's nice and all, but the reader probably won't be back for another read.

An ending happens organically. Like a relationship, you can try to dictate when a couple will experience their first kiss, first fight, first sexual experience, and move toward love or commitment. But you don't really know how any of that will occur until the story unfolds, piece by piece, and you see it as an organic whole.

You know how something terrible happens to you—like a lost job or the end of a relationship—and in the moment, you panic, stress, and scream because you cannot understand why? *Why?* We kneel to God or fate or our loved ones, and we say, "This makes no sense. Why is this happening?"

write naked

Then, later, maybe months or years, we see exactly why and how that event led us to the present. It all clicks into place like one big puzzle. When you are working on how an individual piece fits, it's extremely hard to trust that the entire puzzle will come together in perfect symmetry.

Such is the end of a romance or women's fiction novel (or, any genre). Whether the ending is bittersweet, funny, or happy, the building blocks leading up to it must be in place.

That's when you know you have an ending.

In my novel, *Any Time, Any Place*, my heroine, Raven, holds a secret from my hero, Dalton. Dalton's mother was killed in a car crash when he was young, and the scandal ripped through the town because she was running away with another man. The fallout traumatized Dalton, and he blamed the man for seducing and killing his mother.

Raven's father is the one who ran away with Dalton's mother. Raven has also been tortured by the mysterious circumstances and is hungry for information about Dalton's family to see if she can find the truth.

Dalton is hired to restore the bar in her restaurant and pursues her romantically. Raven decides to use his interest to gain information on the Pierce family. Of course, they end up falling in love, and when the secret is revealed, Dalton feels betrayed and leaves Raven. When she tries to heal things between them, he destroys her in a very intimate scene, choosing to allow the past dictate the future. His brothers finally help him realize that he needs to forgive his mother for abandoning him in order to forgive Raven and allow himself to love again.

The relationships between the parents and the hero and heroine build toward the ending. When Dalton finally finds a letter detailing the facts of his mother's abandonment, he is able to release the past. It takes a long time for Raven to forgive him, but eventually they are able to heal and move forward. Once Dalton forgave his mother, I knew my ending was near, because his entire journey had been building throughout the book. I used a combination of character growth and theme to deliver a satisfying ending.

Theme always needs to hold true for an ending. With *Any Time, Any Place*, forgiveness was at the heart of both relationships and delivered my theme. You must ask if you have carried theme through the story and into the ending. The reader needs to feel like she's eaten a three-course, five-star meal and cannot eat another bite. She is *full*. Full from the story she's invested her time in. She may not recognize that you subtly threaded theme from chapter one all the way to the end, wrapping it up in one big conclusion, but readers don't need to know the mechanics and the steps of a great book.

We do.

Writing well and true are the most important elements in a successful career, from beginnings to endings. I've shared a lot of information here. In all my years of writing, I've made mistakes, experienced triumphs, cried painful tears, and loved this career with every cell in my body. It is the reason I have a full and meaningful life.

I don't know everything and would never pretend to, but writer to writer, we understand each other. We are the same. Our lives have unraveled in a way no one other than another writer could appreciate or understand. This book is over thirty years in the making, written for one reason: The hope that even one tiny segment or chapter can help another writer. The road of the writer is beautiful, yet lonely. When we think of the many individuals who walk beside us on this thoughtful journey, it can make all the difference.

I've talked a lot about writing craft, the writing life, and writing practices. I've spoken about writing philosophies, fears, aspirations, demons, and angels.

But I hope I've delivered my complete theme and message for this book about being a writer.

Magic. Grace. Joy. Wonder.

Writing is … everything.

Being a writer is an important job because we bring emotion and imagination into a world filled with endless, inane chatter. The social media and technological industries may be cutting edge, but when a person stops to read a story—any type of story—the only things in her head are words that have meaning. These are beautiful, glorious words that talk about the power and fragility of life and the human emotions of hope, love, pain, and glory.

This is our job. This is what we must protect at all costs, and it begins by protecting our work and ourselves. We must believe in our stories and ourselves; we must believe in the healing power of words and their ability to touch a part of the human soul that is all too often closed. It's a gift that comes with the high price of work and the potential for failure, rejection, and pain. But it's also bursting with gusts of power and emotion that make it all worthwhile.

Trust in your gift. To protect it and grow, you must write. Every single day you will be confronted by the same obstacles, and every single day you must battle the same demons to get the words on the page. Your story is unique; it's a footprint that no one else can copy, because like a snowflake, there can be no one else that views the world in the exact way you do.

I have had many great mentors in my life. One of them comes from the successful stories of Star Wars—Jedi Master, Yoda.

From the bottom of my heart, I wish all of you talented, worthy, powerful writers one thing, words you should repeat every day you take the battle to the computer or notebook.

May the words be with you. Always.

index

write naked